MARGARET ATWOOD: LANGUAGE, TEXT, AND SYSTEM

MARGARET ATWOOD

LANGUAGE, TEXT, AND SYSTEM

Edited by

Sherrill E. Grace

and

Lorraine Weir

UNIVERSITY OF BRITISH COLUMBIA PRESS
VANCOUVER

MARGARET ATWOOD: Language, Text, and System

This book has been published with the help of a grant from the Canada Council.

Canadian Cataloguing in Publication data
1. Atwood, Margaret, 1939-   — Criticism and
interpretation. I. Grace, Sherrill E., 1944-
II. Weir, Lorraine, 1946-
PS8501.T89Z73   C813'.54   C83-091001-8
PR9199.3.A88Z73

ISBN 0-7748-0170-0

Printed in Canada

In Memory of
Susan Wood
(1948-1980)

Contents

Acknowledgements

The editors would like to thank Margaret Atwood for her generous permission to quote from her work and Oxford University Press for permission to quote the complete text of certain poems. To colleagues and students for their support, advice, and discussion we owe special thanks. We would also like to thank The University of British Columbia for financial assistance in preparing the typescript of this volume and Dr. Jane Fredeman for her help on many matters.

Abbreviations

AC	*The Animals in That Country*. Toronto: Oxford University Press, 1968.
BH	*Bodily Harm*. Toronto: McClelland and Stewart, 1981.
CG	*The Circle Game*. Toronto: Anansi, 1966.
DG	*Dancing Girls*. Toronto: McClelland and Stewart, 1977.
EW	*The Edible Woman*. Toronto: McClelland and Stewart, 1969.
JSM	*The Journals of Susanna Moodie*. Toronto: Oxford University Press, 1970.
LBM	*Life Before Man*. Toronto: McClelland and Stewart, 1979.
LO	*Lady Oracle*. Toronto: McClelland and Stewart, 1976.
PP	*Power Politics*. Toronto: Anansi, 1972.
PU	*Procedures for Underground*. Toronto: Oxford University Press, 1970.
Sfg	*Surfacing*. Toronto: McClelland and Stewart, 1972.
Sur	*Survival: A Thematic Guide to Canadian Literature*. Toronto: Anansi, 1972.
THP	*Two-Headed Poems*. Toronto: Oxford University Press, 1978.
TS	*True Stories*. Toronto: Oxford University Press, 1981.
YAH	*You Are Happy*. Toronto: Oxford University Press, 1974.

Introduction

In *The Poetics of Prose*, Tzvetan Todorov writes that the "goal of investigation is the description of the functioning of a literary system, the analysis of its constituent elements, and the discovery of its laws."[1] Embedded within a text, language is a system within a system, just as the text is in relation to the larger system of an author's *oeuvre* and as that *oeuvre* is in relation to the still larger system of the world as text. Each component functions in metonymic relationship to the larger entity of which it is a part. The object of a reading, then, is to "dismantle"[2] the system of the text in order to discover the focal points or nodes which dominate the system. Accordingly, the reading situates itself within the text and refuses the temptation to explain the system by referring to the author's biography.

These are the basic principles which inform *Margaret Atwood: Language, Text, and System*. The nine readings collected here examine different aspects, different focal points within the Atwood system in an ongoing discussion of individual texts and a continuous reading of her larger system. Each contributor approaches his or her task from a different methodological perspective, and we believe that what emerges from such a collective investigation is a sense of the coherence of a system still in process and of the elegant simplicity of its structure. In "Articulating the 'Space Between,' " Sherrill Grace introduces the Atwood system by examining her criticism and its place within a wider "Canadian system." In "Atwood in a Landscape," Lorraine Weir has employed hermeneutic modes of thinking about texts in order to respond to the Atwood system through the use of a succession of philosophical lenses which serve to open the system out. Our contributors' essays have been arranged with this telescoping movement from single to multiple perspectives in mind.

In "From Poetic to Narrative Structures: The Novels of Margaret Atwood," Linda Hutcheon explores the formal and thematic dimensions of Atwood's fiction and analyses the shift from a static, metaphoric structure in *The Edible Woman* to the more specifically narrative strategies of *Life Before Man*. Barbara Blakely offers a phenomenological feminist reading of the poetry (including *True Stories*) and investigates questions concerning self-definition and the nature of male/female relationships raised in and by the poems. Where Blakely provides a wide-ranging perspective on the poetry in terms of social and cultural concerns, Eli Mandel focuses upon a more restricted sampling of poems and considers "techniques of demystification" in Atwood's poetry. In doing so, he extends to "Atwood's Poetic Politics" his earlier argument from *Another Time*. Robert Cluett's is the most narrowly focused of the essays. While many readers of Atwood's work recognize the central importance of her language, Cluett is the first to subject a single text to detailed stylistic examination. Using computer analysis, "Surface Structures: The Syntactic Profile of *Surfacing*" describes the "truly distinctive" feature of the text as a "reduction of syntactic coloration" rare in the history of English prose.

The next three essays investigate the Atwood system within broader contexts. Anthropologist Marie-Françoise Guédon provides a study of the nature, function, and significance of Indian themes and shamanism in *Surfacing*. Providing a rich background of material on Algonkian tradition, Guédon considers the ethnological side of some of the "techniques of demystification" discussed to quite different ends in Eli Mandel's essay. In his comparative essay, "The Uses of Ambiguity: Margaret Atwood and Hubert Aquin," Philip Stratford describes the function of metaphor and ambiguity in *Surfacing* and *Prochain Episode* and moves through a discussion of the nature of figurative language in these two authors to some observations upon the wider concerns of Québécois and Canadian literatures. George Woodcock's "Metamorphosis and Survival: Notes on the Recent Poetry of Margaret Atwood" is his latest attempt to evaluate a writer who has interested him for many years. Woodcock was one of the first to recognize Atwood's importance and the unity of her "over-reaching vision." Here he reaches back through the Imagists and Romantics to Ovid in order to describe the "poetic excellence," "moral sensitivity," and "intuitive wisdom" of her work.

We thank our contributors for their support and patience with a project which has unexpectedly stretched over several years[3] and for the privilege of using their essays. And we hope that our readers will share our pleasure and sense of challenge as they work with the collection.

S.E.G.
L.W.
Vancouver, September 1982

Notes

1. Tzvetan Todorov, *The Poetics of Prose*, trans. Richard Howard (Ithaca: Cornell University Press, 1977), p. 249.
2. Todorov, *The Poetics of Prose*, p. 237.
3. This collection has been long in preparation. Contributors were at work on their essays and the plans for the volume were complete early in 1980. Although some reference is made to *True Stories*, that volume and *Bodily Harm* appeared after most of the essays were completed.

Articulating the 'Space Between':
Atwood's Untold Stories and Fresh Beginnings

Sherrill E. Grace

Margaret Atwood once wrote that, unlike the empirical British and analytic American, the Canadian "habit of mind . . . is synthetic" and likely to produce "all-embracing systems" which show how particular data fit into "the entire universe."[1] While one might quibble or find exceptions to this tendency — and, of course, Atwood never implies that only a Canadian can have a "synthetic" "habit of mind" — her generalization makes sense for many Canadians and, certainly, for herself. What she is drawing attention to is the importance of coherence through contexts (importance to Canadian philosophers and writers at least), and this sense of coherence, this need to see how an idea or assumption, a word or a symbol, "fits into" a larger system which ideally includes everything is a primary concern of her criticism as well as a constant element in her poetry and fiction. An examination of Atwood's work, first by referring to her context — or part of it — and second, by considering her observations on that context, especially in her criticism, throws some light on Atwood's system as well as on what is characteristically Canadian about her "habit of mind." Because a context of place or region presents special difficulties for Canadian criticism and can result in a reductive approach to art, I prefer to follow S. J. Colman's less problematic example and focus on Atwood's time and her intellectual peers.[2]

For many Canadian writers of Atwood's generation, the 1970's was a decade of confrontation with a growing sense of ideological and philosophical crisis. Two writers, one at the beginning of the decade, one at the end, one a poet, one a philosopher, have been particularly clear about this confrontation. Dennis Lee broke free of a four-years' silence to write *Civil Elegies* (1972) and to begin thinking about *Savage Fields* (1978),[3] and Leslie Armour, reflecting on where Canadians were in the 1970's by examining Canadian philosophy and history, has entitled his latest book, *The Idea of Canada and the Crisis of Community* (1981). Although Lee speaks out of a private sense of crisis and Armour adopts the more public philosopher's stance, what they say and the situations they describe have much in common and not surprisingly they intersect to illuminate aspects of what it means to be Canadian. Using Atwood's definition of literature in *Survival* (p.18), I would say that Lee's poems and literary criticism (if *Savage Fields* can be called that) provide a "mirror," a glimpse into important corners of the Canadian psyche, and Armour's philosophical study provides a "map," a map of history rather than place. Furthermore, this "mirror" and "map" provide a *vade mecum* to Atwood's work and her context, for she describes a similar sense of crisis, charts comparable ideological and moral strategies, and in her definition of the artist strives to mediate between the private and the public domain.

For Lee the crisis stems from his sense of the total failure of the liberal ideology which shapes Western, notably American, life, an ideology founded upon the bifurcation of consciousness and matter, of subjective value and will and objective facts, and supporting the struggle for complete domination of "earth" by "world."[4] Moreover, Lee holds out little hope for a reconstruction of these epistemological and ideological models (which he describes as suicidal in *Savage Fields*), because "the cosmology of strife is still trapped within the bankruptcy provoked by liberalism, in that it apparently cannot articulate any other way of being."[5] Although Lee distinguishes between the dualistic model of "savage fields" and the classic dichotomies of liberalism, he nevertheless depicts humanity as trapped by both systems so that even the texts he identifies as literature of the "savage field" (*The Collected Works of Billy the Kid* and *Beautiful Losers*) do nothing more than articulate a "grammar of the intolerable." And yet, paradoxically, the problem that began for Lee with the recognition that as a colonized Canadian he could neither accept American values and assumptions nor identify distinct Canadian ones developed into the densely elaborated conception of "savage fields": in other words, to a degree Lee himself managed to speak the silence of his colonized space, and in doing so he used the contradictions and divisions — personal and historical — at the heart of the Canadian identity: in *Savage Fields* he wrote a very Canadian book — tenacious, "synthetic" (in Atwood's sense), and obsessed with duality.

In *The Idea of Canada*, Armour approaches a problem similar to the one which disturbs Lee — the "conflict between our inherited notions of an organic society and our confrontations with the technologically-based individualism associated with the economies of the contemporary west" — but his vision of Canada, and of the philosophical options open to mankind, is more hopeful.[6] Armour starts with the assumption, not only that we must, but that we can discover a theory which preserves history and traditional values while providing at the same time a model for a society which is flexible and pluralistic. To do so is to articulate the "space between"[7] the extremes of an American liberal individualist like John Rawls and a systematic collectivist like Marx. To do so is to articulate a typically Canadian "habit of mind." Like Lee, Armour begins his search for a theory with the paradoxes of Canadian history and the wider Cartesian dilemma. Both English- and French-Canadian philosophers, he argues, have resisted "the Cartesian mentality" and have seen nature neither as conquerable "American sunshine" nor as Romantic landscape. Men like Louis Lachance, John Watson, John Murray, and Jacob Sherman all sought a vision, to one degree or another, pluralistic and communitarian, and it is this philosophic position — revering history, suspicious of American individualism and high capitalist liberal ideology, and resistant to subject/object dichotomies — which, according to Armour, comprises a distinctly Canadian tradition. One conclusion to be drawn from Armour's study is that the general ignorance of this tradition has compounded the problems for those Canadians who, Armour writes, almost as if in response to Lee or Atwood, "feel bewildered without a vision that can fit the pieces together."[8] Armour's answer to the problem of a national identity crisis begins with the recognition of a *Canadian* tradition, in history, philosophy, politics, a tradition that is "synthetic," resilient, shared by many Canadian communities, and quite distinct from American traditions.

Like Lee and Armour, Atwood has responded deeply to this sense of crisis; like them she has re-examined the philosophic and ideological bases of modern North American life, and like them she has tried, most obviously in *Survival* (1972), to identify a Canadian tradition and "habit of mind." What Armour has perhaps overlooked in his claim that *Survival* exaggerates the presence of a Cartesian mentality in Canadian literature is that *Survival* rejects the bifurcation of reality which permits an ideology of "power politics," of strife and domination. In fact, from the beginning of her career, Atwood has tried to find a third way, a non-Cartesian way, to think of and structure images of personal and social life. In a manner which strikes me as particularly "Canadian" (from its assumptions to its tentative resolutions), she has constantly struggled to articulate Armour's "space between."[9] For this reason, I think, Lee cannot include much of her work in his theory of "savage fields" and, therefore, must describe her writing as "liberation literature . . . possessed by its own coherence."[10] As shown below, Atwood's system is closer to the one Armour describes than to the despair of Lee's "savage fields." Even in *Bodily Harm* and "Notes Towards a Poem That Can Never Be Written" from *True Stories*, where she confronts one of the most terrifying crises faced by all men in our time, Atwood refuses to be silenced by the "space between," and she consistently affirms the power of language to fill the gap, to create a third way of being out of the either/or alternatives which her system resists and at moments negates.

As might be expected, the principle of coherence is important to Atwood. In an article on W. D. Valgardson's fiction, she examines the popular misconception that the best writers "grow," and her observations are relevant here:

It's a critical fallacy of our times, derived perhaps from psychology or optimistic self-help books, that a writer should "grow," "change," or "develop." This fallacy causes us to demand the same kind of behavior from writers that we expect from children or radishes: "grow," or there's something wrong with you. But writers are not radishes. If you look at what most writers actually do, it resembles a theme with variations more than it does the popular notion of growth. Writers' universes may become more elaborate, but they do not necessarily become essentially different.[11]

Atwood's "universe," or system, is not something that has changed in the sense of having altered or become essentially different. It was there from the earliest poems (in *Double Persephone*, 1961), waiting to be articulated, beginning to be imaged.

Much criticism to date has distorted or ignored this coherence. Certain of her works have been adopted by nationalists in Canada, who emphasize *Survival* and *The Journals of Susanna Moodie*, and by feminists in the United States, who focus upon *Power Politics, Surfacing*, and the subsequent novels, but both groups tend to ignore the common roots of these aspects of Atwood's writing. However, recent criticism, here and in the United States, has begun to examine some of the elements which are fundamental to all her work and, therefore, constitute the basis of her system.

One element of her work which is frequently emphasized by critics is the theme of duality or polarity, what Gloria Onley calls Atwood's "cartesian hell."[12] However, the fact that duality is more than thematic (expressed in contents or subject matter), and that Atwood is not simply rejecting duality but working with it, from it, cannot be overemphasized. A second key element is her treatment of nature (as setting, image, and code), and what she means or implies by "natural," provokes the most discussion or — on the part of some feminists — concern.[13] Moreover, prior to *Two-Headed Poems* (as the following essays by Blakely and Weir point out) Atwood manipulates the inescapable tension between the artificial and the natural, a tension not merely destructive but also dynamic, a tension which enlists language in the process of recognizing and healing the polarities and divisions of a "cartesian hell." The central importance of the self is another element in her work that has been recognized, but what Atwood means by *self*, or how this concept relates to or influences other aspects of her art is less well understood.[14] Finally, there can be little doubt about the importance of the fourth element in this discussion of the Atwood system: language. Frank Davey was perhaps the first to point out that Atwood perceives the word, like space, stereotypes, and myths, as a potential trap, and that her poems can be traps when the artifact freezes the temporal processes of life and creativity.[15] But what is always challenging about Atwood's use of language is her continuing exploration (and exploitation) of its dangerous power.

Through an analysis of these four elements, duality, nature, self, and language, it is possible to describe Atwood's system. By system a structuralist refers to the set of codes that structure a writer's work. These codes are present in the work linguistically, or as configurations of images, characters, actions, and so on. Because I am interested in the relations within or between texts, which can be viewed as metonymies in an artistic and ideological process, I am primarily concerned here with Atwood's use of cultural codes, and with the system of values or ethical position that directs her art and illuminates how and why she articulates the "space between." Atwood's system, in this sense, is not a static but a dynamic process in which the works constitute a coherent argument, a dialectic (which is closer to Marx than Hegel because it eschews transcendence), while each individual text functions dynamically, moving through a series of poetic or narrative strategies — as Hutcheon points out in her essay. Furthermore, Atwood identifies human failure as acquiescence in those Western dichotomies which postulate the inescapable, static division of the world into hostile opposites: culture/nature, male/female, straight line/curved space, head/body, reason/instinct, victor/victim. Indeed, one of the defining qualities of *Surfacing*, as Stratford explains, is Atwood's rejection of stasis in favour of a dynamic third way. *Surfacing* is not, either linguistically or thematically, what Lee would call "savage fields" literature articulating a "grammar of the intolerable."

Although Atwood attempts to overcome dichotomies creatively in the poetry and fiction, her description of this divided world and of the literature produced in such a world is clearest in her criticism, especially in *Survival*. In fact, her criticism tells us a great deal about her own system — she describes *Survival* as, among other things, a "cross between a personal statement . . . and a political manifesto" (*Sur*, p. 13) — and it is an appropriate place to turn for information about her views on art and culture, and on the perceptions, relations and influences which condition each.

Survival: A Thematic Guide to Canadian Literature, is an amusing, highly readable, perceptive study, less of "themes" (a term which is misleading), than of patterns in Canadian literature. These, Atwood argues, arise out of a specific historical, socio-political, and economic context. Canada perceives itself as a collective victim, she maintains, because Canada has been a colony, exploited and oppressed economically, with certain describable mental and cultural side-effects that inevitably condition its literature. Atwood is, in fact, presenting in *Survival* what Rick Salutin rightly describes as a "proto-" or "pre-Marxist" argument, a type of "prolegomenon to a Marxist criticism of Canadian literature."[16] As Salutin goes on to say, the theory of survival is "highly dialectical" and "practical"; it "establishes a causal connection between a culture and the economic foundations of the society in which the culture is found."[17]

There are other dialectical aspects of Atwood's criticism besides this basic materialist one, most notably her views about the dialectical relationship between a culture and its art and the method for achieving change within each sphere of activity. Underlying her critical writing, from reviews and articles to *Survival*, is the basic assumption that there is a dynamic generated between an artist and his society, and she states this point clearly in her defence of *Survival* against Robin Matthews:

> Far from thinking of writers as totally isolated individuals, I see them as inescapably connected with their society. The nature of the connection will vary — the writer may unconsciously reflect the society, he may consciously examine it and project ways of changing it; and the connection between writer and society will increase in intensity as the society . . . becomes the "subject" of the writer.[18]

This assumption enables Atwood to insist upon the possibility of change being effected, at least in small part, by the critic and artist who attempt to examine a society through the patterns which its literature has produced (and is producing), and who, at the same time, refuse to accept those patterns as unalterable constants, insisting instead on seeing them as manifestations of a historical process and socio-cultural dynamic. At the same time as she maintains her commitment to these dialectical principles, Atwood also believes that "the primary duty of the writer is to the thing being made."[19] This duty, reinforced by her fascination with gothicisms, ghosts, monsters, myths, and prose romance, both nineteenth century (Rider Haggard) and contemporary (P. K. Page, Iris Murdoch, Gwendolyn Mac-Ewen and Marie-Claire Blais),[20] suggests that she believes imagination to be a mysterious power and the work of art, *free* in some way, of social conditioning, if not fully autonomous. On the one hand then, art seems independent of its culture, while on the other, it is shaped by its culture; either way, it mirrors or maps that culture.

Somewhat cynically, Atwood describes this ambivalent attitude as a "buffer zone" position:

> if you agree . . . that language and form are important, Art moves in mysterious ways and cannot be trammelled by definitions imposed by social theory . . . and if you also agree . . . that yes, there is a relationship between the society and the art it produces . . . you begin to feel like those countries called "buffer zones" in the history books: whichever way you face you'll be labelled as being on the other side.[21]

But the paradox, or contradiction, is only apparent: as several of the essays in this volume make clear, system and text for Atwood, like language itself, are not creators of a separate, autonomous world — naming alone does not make a thing real — nor are they slavish imitators of a distinct and separate reality; from a phenomenological view-point, language (as *parole* or as the extended discourse of a text),[22] is shaped by the experienced world as much as it shapes, names, or orders the world:

> Language, like the mouths
> that hold and release
> it, is wet & living, each
>
> word is wrinkled
> with age, swollen
> with other words, with blood, smoothed by the numberless
> flesh tongues that have passed across it.
>
> (*THP*, p. 67)

In Atwood's definition, literature functions as a mirror in which the reader can see himself and his world, if he learns how to *see*. But literature "is not only a mirror, it is also a map, a geography of the mind" (*Sur*, pp. 18–19). *Survival* is a description of that mirror, which Atwood designates as *Canadian* literature, and an *Atwoodian* guide to the reading of that map. It is an analysis and interpretation, not of subject matter, but of the characteristic patterns given to a subject, of shape, structure, system (*Sur*, p. 237). Thus, man's struggle with a winter landscape may be a theme, but images of obdurate resistance resulting in victimization of either man or landscape create a pattern and stand in metonymic relation to a system.

Atwood begins her consideration of Canadian literary systems in *Survival* by suggesting that every culture has "a single unifying and informing symbol at its core" (*Sur*, p. 31), and that this "symbol" — be it expressed as

> word, phrase, idea, image or all of these — functions like a system of beliefs (it *is* a system of beliefs, though not always a formal one) which holds the country together. (*Sur*, p. 31)

For Canada, she argues, this symbol is survival, but is there such a symbol for the Atwood system? I think there is and have called it, quoting Atwood, "violent duality."[23] With Atwood, however, duality must be understood as dynamic, not static, because she is concerned, not simply with the fact of Western dichotomies, but with the process of overcoming the polarization of world and self, as well as the hierarchical power structures which such divisions produce. Reminiscent of those philosophers whom Armour describes as representative of the Canadian tradition, her dualistic system functions to break down the boundaries separating victor/victim, mind/body, self/other, and culture/nature of the Cartesian model and to establish the presence of an all-inclusive dynamic process based upon connection and continuity between and among dichotomies. As Stratford notes in his discussion of metaphor and Hutcheon remarks in her examination of narrative, Atwood's art pushes through stasis towards process. And it is precisely this process which Atwood evokes in "You did it":

> When will you learn
> the flame and the wood/flesh
> it burns are whole and the same?

(*PP*, p. 32)

Merely to transform culture into nature, victor into victim, is to remain trapped within the pointless, static system of dichotomies.

Hence, the four victim positions in the survival system are not static states (only the critical model is static, *Sur*, p. 40), but stages, within a process that points on to the fourth position which is itself grounded in process:

> From Position Four, man himself is seen as part of the process; he does not define himself as "good" or "weak" as against a hostile Nature, or as "bad" or "aggressive" as against a passive, powerless Nature. He can accept his own body, including its sexuality, as part of this process, accepting too the versatility that the process requires. Since he does not see life as something that can only be maintained inside a fortress and at the expense of shutting out Nature and sex, he is free to move *within* space rather than in a self-created tank *against* it. (*Sur*, p. 63)

Clearly, according to Atwood, the writer assists in the description and establishment of this dynamic system by creating those mirrors and maps which show people who and where they are and by urging them, to one degree or another, to recognize or even alter their state. However, the reader, too, must be an active agent in this process — to read is as much a creative act as to write.[24]

Given the destructive nature of the static model of dichotomies that fosters and relies upon hierarchical power structures, how does Atwood suggest that one can break free from political, psychological, and sexual victor/victim postures (while at the same time retaining, instead of transcending, opposites) in order to establish a dualistic system grounded in continuity and process? How does one articulate the "space between" these extremes? How does one learn that "the flame and the wood/flesh / it burns are whole and the same?" *Survival* offers an answer to these questions by analysing the static system of polarities as it manifests itself thematically in Canadian literature. Of the thematic patterns which she discusses, two are especially significant for her system: the perceived hostile opposition between culture and nature, and the separation between self and other.

The determining assumptions of Western culture rest upon the continuing separation and opposition of the human and non-human, of consciousness and matter, which allow man to subjugate and exploit nature, thereby denying its independent existence and the value of its "otherness." Although this attitude characterizes male/female oppositions as well as theories about the individual psyche, in *Survival* Atwood discusses it primarily within the national context of discovering, pioneering, and settling a country. Canada, she argues, was founded upon the belief that a specific order was inherent in the universe. Hence,

> Canadian settler figures are less likely [than Americans] to see their activities as the construction of a new world built according to their free fancies than the implementation of an order that is "right." The imposition of the straight line on the curve tends to get seen by those doing the imposing as part of the Divine Plan, and that can lead to a good deal of intolerance and rigidity. (*Sur*, p. 122)

By casting himself as the "square man in a round whole" in the belief that he must impose his reason, order, culture, in the form of straight lines, upon an utterly separate, disordered, irrational force known as Nature, the pioneer causes havoc in one of two ways: if he wins the battle with nature, he will destroy something essentially human which he has also denied; if he loses the battle, he will be overwhelmed by a world he has not understood and will be driven insane.

Atwood is more interested in the ramifications of the first possibility, and often her images of ecological destruction (the blue heron in *Surfacing*, for example) function as metaphors for man's destruction of the natural aspect of himself, or of woman perceived as part of nature. The one point in *Survival* at which she refers to her own poetry is in her discussion of explorations of the opposition between culture/nature or straight line and curve. "I tend to be on the side of the curve," she remarks:

> and I haven't yet decided whether that stance is Position Two defeatism (don't build a fence because it will fall down anyway) or Position Four acceptance of life-as-process (don't build a fence because you'll be keeping out things you should be letting in). (*Sur*, p. 124)

Most of her writing, including *Survival*, is in neither position. Instead, it seems focused upon those very fences in the effort to tear them down. Where she comes closest to Position Four — in certain poems such as "A Place: Fragments" (*The Circle Game*), "A Book of Ancestors" (*You Are Happy*), several poems in *Two-Headed Poems*, and at the end of *Surfacing* — she does so by immersing her character or speakers in nature or in images of the natural, of life-as-process ("open yourself like this and become whole," *YAH*, p. 96). As she suggests in her essay "Canadian Monsters," man re-possesses himself through "an entry into the forest," and this can lead to an awareness, at least, of a dynamic dualistic system.[25] Another way of approaching Position Four is to follow native Indian cosmology which can serve as the necessary model for a more integrated, holistic view of life. However, neither in *Survival* nor *Surfacing*, nor in specific poems, does Atwood advocate White adoption of Indian history or individuals; as Guédon indicates, it is the Indian system, their way of being and seeing, that interests her.

Predictably, Atwood's tendency to be on the side of nature, as well as her increasingly apparent reverence for the earth and biological processes (present in *The Animals in That Country, The Journals of Susanna Moodie*, and *Surfacing*, but clearest in *Two-Headed Poems*), has been the focal point of feminist debate about her work, especially in the United States. Too close an identification of the female with nature can become a trap that limits and defines woman in terms of what Simone de Beauvoir terms the "Other," the exploited and devalued force in the culture/nature dichotomy. Broadly or narrowly defined, culture then tends to become the preserve of the male, an arena that excludes female presence or power. The danger inherent in siding with the loser in this victor/victim struggle is obvious.

One of the most thoughtful American studies of this nature-woman identification is Carol P. Christ's theological-feminist reading of *Surfacing*. Christ argues that Atwood's perception of the natural dynamic, together with her ability to create such an intimate sense of identification with natural powers in *Surfacing*, may reflect a uniquely female response, not only to nature, to plants and animals, but to life and human relationships. Christ concludes that *Surfacing*

> suggests that the opposition of spirit and body, nature and person, which is endemic in Western culture, is neither necessary nor salutary. Her novel suggests that spiritual insight surfaces through attention to the body, and that the achievement of authentic selfhood and power depends on understanding one's grounding in nature and natural energies.[26]

Pursuing a rather different line in her feminist essay for this volume, Blakely goes further than Christ to suggest that by the time of *Two-Headed Poems* Atwood no longer anatomizes destructive dichotomies, what Christ calls "the opposition of spirit and body, nature and person," but instead celebrates "matriarchal guides." Whether or not Atwood would claim that her position in *Surfacing* or *Two-Headed Poems* is uniquely female, her commitment to the principle of "one's grounding in nature and natural energies" (as Christ expresses it), as well as her celebration of "matriarchal guides," is emphatic throughout these poems. She prays to a "Black Stone Mother God" and salutes her dying grandmother, "mother / of my mother, old bone / tunnel through which I came" (*THP*, p. 40). In "All Bread" she reminds us that recognizing our connection with the earth, with "natural energies," leads to consecration, "almost":

> Lift these ashes
> into your mouth, your blood;
> to know what you devour
> is to consecrate it,
> almost. All bread must be broken
> so it can be shared. Together
> we eat this earth.
>
> (*THP*, p. 109)

The second crucial dichotomy that Atwood explores is that of self/other, and in this case, as in the culture/nature opposition, she strives to break down the static condition of mutual exclusiveness separating these opposites. Beginning with "This is a Photograph of Me," Atwood singles out the visual as the sense most guilty of maintaining the illusion of radical separation between the I and not-I, be it nature or another human being; hence, the importance of eye and mirror imagery, as well as the significant visual dimension to so many of her poems. But perhaps the best point from which to approach Atwood's understanding of the self/other opposition is from her concept of the self, because from this concept grows her sense of the nature and purpose of the creative act.

Whether manifestations of this sense of self are examined in certain poems ("Pre-Amphibian" and "The Settlers" from *The Circle Game*, "Progressive Insanities of a Pioneer" from *The Animals in That Country*, most of the *Journals*, "Fishing for Eel Totems" from *Procedures for Underground*, "You did it" from *Power Politics* and "Book of Ancestors" from *You Are Happy*, for example), or in *Surfacing* where the speaker becomes "a place," it is apparent that Atwood views the self as co-extensive with the environment. She briefly discussed this view during a reading of her poetry when she distinguished between self and ego: to define self as ego is to posit absolute separation between a conscious subject and its object; such a view leads to the projection of a static, hierarchic system of dichotomies upon all non-ego, if not to a destructive solipsism. But to define the self phenomenologically, as Atwood does — as a place in which things happen, where experiences intersect[27] — is to facilitate a harmoniously integrated system of complementary, interdependent elements, functioning together continually to produce a whole that is more than its parts, a system where everything "fits in." Furthermore, such a view suggests that the self is neither the product nor the solipsistic creator of the world, but a function of the process of relationship.

According to Atwood, language is instrumental in maintaining an awareness of mutual interdependence of self and world. For example, in a discussion of John Newlove's poetry, Atwood describes his strong sense of entrapment in a negative world of things, and then goes on to connect this sense of the world with an attitude towards self and language:

Because the self and the corner are connected and possibly synonymous, the way out of the corner is the way out of the self. If everything outside the self, including other people, is postulated as negative or devoid of reality, one may as well stay in the self; it at least is known, which is some comfort, and one can have dreams and fantasies there. But if there is a "truth" to which words in some way correspond, then the encounter with the outside world through words, the externalization and transcendence of the self, becomes possible.[28]

Words, then, can free an individual from the tyranny of self-as-ego because words and texts, that "liquid and effortless" song (*THP*, 75), can force him to acknowledge his connection with a world which he shapes and by which he is shaped. Through words Atwood can persuade her reader to accept her new landscape of untold stories and fresh beginnings. Indeed, through the power of her "poetic language,"[29] shattering the constraints of rationalist discourse in order to release the rhythms and emotions of a semiotic process, she articulates the space, not only between Rawls and Marx, but also between self and nature and between self-as-ego and self-as-place.

Although one should never ask, as Atwood warns, for the "true story" which is, after all, a deception, stories (or poems) have power, and the quality of despair — personal and more general — that colours so many of the poems in *True Stories*, is held firmly in check by her belief in words, in their ability to communicate and make visible, to demystify (as Eli Mandel demonstrates) experience: "A word after a word/after a word is power" (*TS*, p. 64). And this belief in poetry, which is both a "mouthful of dirt" (*TS*, p. 93) and "a prayer" (*TS*, p. 99), is a calmly desperate one, even *here*:

> Elsewhere, this poem is not invention,
> Elsewhere, this poem takes courage.
> Elsewhere, this poem must be written
> because the poets are already dead. . . .
>
> Elsewhere you must write this poem
> because there is nothing more to do.

(*TS*, p. 70)

Just as Atwood's definition of the self arises out of centuries of Western religious and philosophical debate, so too her aesthetics and the ethics of her system are familiar. Continuity, context, process, harmoniously functioning relationship, reliance upon natural and biological forms — together these principles generate Atwood's system. It would be a mistake, however, to suggest that Atwood develops this system in her work as a way of resolving her own ideological and aesthetic confusions or conflicts.[30] Her aesthetic and philosophic position, as well as her ideology, appear to be deliberately and self-consciously related, and her system is "organic" and "pluralistic," much like the "idea of a society" which, Armour suggests, "has very old roots in Canada" — a system and a society where "the parts work together to form an intelligible whole in which each has a unique place."[31] Beginning with the dominant Western system of hierarchical dichotomies which support economic and class structures and encode a society's political, cultural, and psychological values, she continually explores the evils of that system, forcing her readers to recognize their blindness and responsibility. To acquiesce in victimization, whether psychological as in *Surfacing* or physical as in *Bodily Harm* (and Atwood insists that the two are inseparable), is to accept as real the illusion of passivity. As she reminds us at the end of *Survival*, we can "escape from our old habits of looking at things, and [re-create] a new way of seeing, experiencing and imaging — or imagining — which we ourselves have helped to shape" (p. 246).

What she continues to offer is a system embodying dualities, but dualities understood as mutually interdependent aspects of a continuum of relationship, functioning dialectically and modelled upon natural life processes. The walls and fences which are set up to divide culture from nature, male from female, logic from intuition, and which facilitate domination and devaluation, must come down, not in order to change a culture-male-logic dominated system into its opposite, but to facilitate the harmonious process of inter-relationship. Hence, to read Atwood correctly is to understand her as breaking imprisoning circles, not as resolving (cancelling or transcending) polarities altogether, not as transforming myth into reality or as reversing the power structures in the dichotomous system. Even nature, while clearly depicted as curved, positive, and closely identified with female processes, can never replace or dominate culture; at the end of *Surfacing* the narrator will go back because she is human. Only from *within* the system of culture/nature and male/female dichotomies can Atwood's system be described, in any pejorative sense, as predominantly "natural" or "female."

Although there are several points in her work where Atwood emphasizes harmonious relationship instead of repeated exploration of polarity — for example, as early as "A Place: Fragments" from *The Circle Game* — *Two-Headed Poems* is, to date, the volume which most deliberately celebrates natural processes, connections, and continuities. Formally and thematically, these poems establish simple continuities through serial form, historical and personal subjects (notably mother/daughter relationships), and sensuous imagery (eyes, those most untrustworthy organs, are much less important here than touch and smell). Is this Atwood writing from "Position Four acceptance of life-as-process"? According to *Survival*, insofar as a writer is connected with his society, writing from "Position

Four" is impossible until that society has been changed. And yet, Atwood has done more than merely describe the parameters of the "cartesian hell," more than dramatize and warn against its dangers. Lee is right: she does not, for the most part, articulate a "grammar of the intolerable." Instead, she struggles to free herself, her readers, and her forms from the potentially imprisoning spaces of ideology, self, and artifact. The tension generated by this struggle is fundamental to the energy and success of her work, to what seems virtually an act of faith in *True Stories* and *Bodily Harm*. Through the promise of "a repertoire of untold stories, / a fresh beginning" (*THP*, p. 13), she continues to break the silence by articulating the "space between."

Notes

1. "Eleven Years of Alphabet," *Canadian Literature* 49 (1971): pp. 62–63; Atwood's examples of such systems are those of McLuhan and Frye, and her essay is a tribute to Reaney's efforts to identify a Canadian tradition in *Alphabet*. I am grateful to my colleagues, Laurie Ricou and Graham Good, for their helpful comments on this paper.
2. In "Margaret Atwood, Lucien Goldmann's Pascal, and the Meaning of 'Canada,' " *University of Toronto Quarterly* 48 (1979): 245–62, Colman uses Goldmann's "genetic structuralist" method to analyse Atwood's "world-view," as manifested in *Surfacing* and to relate that view to her social group of intellectuals and publicists. Colman's conclusion is twofold: first, that "we" and "Canada" in Atwood's work are synonymous with this *partis pris* group which dislikes American models and influence but is uncertain about Canadian ones; second, that *Surfacing* expresses Goldmann's "tragic world-view," which depicts man as caught between contradictory and irreconcilable claims. By comparing Atwood's views with some specific examples from this peer group (which Colman does not do), it will be possible to qualify the latter conclusion: Atwood is closer to the dialectical world-view than the tragic. Colman's restrictions on the meaning of "Canada," though interesting, do not seem conclusive.
3. Lee describes this crisis, and the context for it, in "Cadence, Country, Silence: Writing in Colonial Space," *Boundary* 2, 3 (1974): 151-68.
4. *Savage Fields: An Essay in Literature and Cosmology* (Toronto: Anansi, 1977). In particular, see pp. 8–11 and Lee's description of "liberal cosmology," pp. 49–56.
5. Lee, *Savage Fields*, p. 118. Lee has managed to break the silence, verging on self-pity, described in "Cadence, Country, Silence," but in *Savage Fields* his vision is circular and negative — in fact, a better example of Goldmann's "tragic world-view" than *Surfacing*.
6. *The Idea of Canada and the Crisis of Community* (Ottawa: Steel Rail Publishing, 1981), p. xiv.
7. Ibid., p. xiv.
8. Ibid., p. 24.
9. Armour suggests (p. 23) that in *Survival* Atwood fails to recognize traditional Canadian resistance to the Cartesian mentality and, therefore, that she describes Canadian writers as hostile to nature. Although it is true that Atwood emphasizes examples of a harsh destructive nature in Canadian literature in order to illustrate her survival thesis, it is a misreading of her theory of process to claim that, as a result, her system creates despair. All her work, including *Survival*, rests upon resistance to a Cartesian model, whether or not she explicitly identifies this resistance as part of a Canadian tradition.
10. Lee, *Savage Fields*, pp. 116–17.

11. "Valgardsonland," *Essays on Canadian Writing* 16 (Fall-Winter 1979–80), p. 188.
12. "Power Politics in Bluebeard's Castle," *Canadian Literature* 60 (1974), p. 26. For other essays on Atwood's treatment of duality, see, T. D. MacLulich, "Atwood's Adult Fairy Tale: Lévi-Strauss, Bettelheim, and *The Edible Woman*," *Essays on Canadian Writing* 2 (1978), pp. 111–29, and Frank Davey, "Atwood's Gorgon Touch," *Studies in Canadian Literature* (1977), pp. 146–63.
13. For a discussion of nature and natural forms in Atwood, see Gloria Onley's "Power Politics in Bluebeard's Castle" and the following feminist studies: Carol P. Christ, "Margaret Atwood: The Surfacing of Women's Spiritual Quest and Vision," *Signs* 2 (1976), pp. 316–30 and "Refusing to be a Victim" in *Diving Deep and Surfacing: Women Writers on Spiritual Quest* (Boston, 1980), pp. 41–53; Judith Plaskow, "On Carol Christ on Margaret Atwood: Some Theological Reflections," *Signs* 2 (1976), pp. 331–39; Barbara Hill Rigney, *Madness and Sexual Politics in the Feminist Novel: Studies in Brontë, Woolf, Lessing and Atwood* (Madison: University of Wisconsin Press, 1978).
14. Although there is considerable room for disagreement with her conclusion that *Surfacing* ends in narcissism, Rosemary Sullivan offers perceptive comments on Atwood's handling of the self-not-self dichotomy in "Breaking the Circle," *Malahat Review* 41 (1977): 30–31.
15. Frank Davey, "Atwood's Gorgon Touch."
16. "A Note on the Marxism of Atwood's *Survival*," *Malahat Review* 41 (1977): 57.
17. Ibid., pp. 58–59.
18. "Surviving the Critics: Matthews and Misrepresentation," *This Magazine is about Schools* 7 (1973), p. 33. Salutin also refers to this passage, and goes on to point out that "*Survival* is a 'moment' in the dialectic of Canadian society — and knows itself to be so."
19. "A Reply," *Signs* 2 (1976): 340.
20. Atwood began graduate work on Rider Haggard and has published one study of his novel *She*, "Superwoman Drawn and Quartered: The Early Forms of *She*," *Alphabet* 10 (1965), pp. 65–82. Other essays in which she discusses Gothic and Romance conventions include: "Introduction" to *The Sun and the Moon* by P. K. Page (Toronto: Anansi, 1973) in which she groups Page's novel together with *The Blithedale Romance, Zanoni, She, Tay John*, MacEwen's prose and Blais' *Mad Shadows*; "Masterful: A game of musical beds in a house of mirrors," a review of Iris Murdoch's *The Sacred and Profane Love Machine* in the *Globe and Mail*, 1 June 1974, p. 23; and, "Canadian Monsters: Some Aspects of the Supernatural in Canadian Fiction," in *The Canadian Imagination*, ed. David Staines (Cambridge, MA.: Harvard University Press, 1977), pp. 97–122.
21. "Poetry in the Buffer Zone," *Times Literary Supplement*, 26 October 1973, pp. 1305–6.
22. The distinction between *langue/parole*, as well as the dialectical relationship between them, are commonplaces of Saussurean semiotic theory clearly summarized by Roland Barthes in *Elements of Semiology*, trans. Annette Lavers and Colin Smith (New York: Hill & Wang, 1968).
23. *Violent Duality: A Study of Margaret Atwood* (Montreal: Véhicule Press, 1980). Surely "survival" and "violent duality" are two sides of the same coin — surviving through violent duality — and to see them as such obviates the need to castigate *Survival* for being a personal obsession disguised as criticism of a national literature.
24. See Linda Hutcheon's argument on this point, pp. 29-30.
25. Atwood, "Canadian Monsters," in *The Canadian Imagination*, p. 114.
26. "Margaret Atwood: The Surfacing of Women's Spiritual Quest and Vision," p. 330.
27. Atwood describes her view in the introductory remarks to a reading of the poetry on the cassette by High Barnet, Toronto, 1973.
28. "How Do I Get Out of Here: The Poetry of John Newlove," *Open Letter* 4 (Spring 1973): 66.
29. By "poetic language" Julia Kristeva means that discourse which disrupts the "symbolic" function of language, represented in syntax, sign, and nomination, by stressing such "semiotic" operations as rhythm and intonation. Kristeva argues that this disruption creates "a dissonance within the thetic, paternal function of language" and is capable of revealing and overriding "the constraints of a civilization dominated by transcendental rationality." See her essay, "From One Identity to An Other," in *Desire in Language*, ed. Leon S. Roudiez, trans. Thomas Gora et al. (New York: Columbia University Press, 1980), particularly pp. 133–40. Kristeva's concept of "poetic language" reveals some interesting aspects of Atwood's style.
30. Terry Eagleton criticizes the various attempts of British writers from Eliot and Dickens to Joyce and

Lawrence to overcome, aesthetically, the historical and ideological contradictions facing them. Combining Marxist and formalist methodologies, he argues that the organic totalizing aesthetic systems of these writers "rationalize the contradictions of [the] historical situation," and he calls for the destruction of such "corporate and organicist" aesthetics. "Ideology and Literary Form," *New Left Review* 90 (1975): 81–109. Atwood's awareness of the historical process, as well as of the relationship between ideology and aesthetics, is especially clear in *Survival*.

31. Armour, *Idea of Canada*, p. xiii. Or as he later points out: "In Canada, although the capitalist system came to us, the individualist ideology did not — or at least not wholly. What we continued to generate, at least in part, was the ideology of the organic society. We did so, of course, in the context of two languages, two sets of institutions, two of almost everything" (p. 79).

2

From Poetic to Narrative Structures:
The Novels of Margaret Atwood

Linda Hutcheon

It has recently been argued that the one undisputed attribute of the modernist temper has proved to be self-consciousness.[1] Margaret Atwood's own self-conscious obsession with the paradoxes of the act of artistic creation in both her prose and her verse has not gone unnoticed by her critics and explicators, though few have ventured to link these aesthetic, formal concerns to her moral thematic issues. This is presumably because they feel, as indeed many have, that such literary introversion somehow precludes the moral orientation of the English novel tradition. Her early use of the short lyric poem has led many[2] to suggest that for Atwood, to write is to fix, to order into a static form. But her increasing concentration on narrative, by nature a more temporal, kinetic art form, should prompt a critical review of this "circle game" interpretation of the "creative process according to Atwood" — both in its formal and in its thematic dimensions. Perhaps it is only the *written* that is fixed; the act of *writing* itself is a dynamic process which, though it can only employ the static counters of language, is capable of being resurrected in the equally dynamic process of reading, the bringing to life of the dead black marks on the white page. Narrative perhaps provides a more appropriate and extended vehicle than the lyric for the aesthetic and moral exploration of the tensions between process and product.

If this hypothesis were to be tested, the first novel published, *The Edible Woman*, would probably be pivotal in the argument: the transition from lyric to narrative would likely be revealed in the treatment of the static/dynamic paradox. And, in fact, this novel is indeed a very highly structured, "circle game" sort of text. More importantly, however, it has proved to be the most densely metaphoric (not symbolic) of her works, on the narrative, if not linguistic level. By this last added qualification, I mean that it is the narrative elements (actions, objects, characters) that take on thematic and moral value through — and sometimes *only* through — their structural role in the novel. By the time Atwood comes to write her fourth novel, *Life Before Man*, this reliance on the ordering patterns of her lyric poems has been integrated into a more complex and more specifically narrative technique that allows the moral dimension of modern self-conscious form to develop fully. The strong ideological impact of *Bodily Harm*, in fact, would probably have been impossible without this progression from poetic to narrative structures.

In *The Edible Woman*, when Duncan informs Marian that hunger is more basic than love (*EW*, p. 100), he not only echoes Schiller's view that the entire conduct of the world is controlled by this duo of appetites, but he also sets up the two thematic poles that will structure this novel, a novel about the various forms and dangers of consumerism and consuming. George Woodcock has seen this as a theme of "emotional cannibalism,"[3] conflating the two poles into one accurate and memorable phrase. But if we choose to retain the separation, we are struck by the fact that the narrative elements begin to order themselves in what has been called a kind of metonymic[4] structure — that is, by contiguity with one or other of the two poles. The "circle game" of inclusion then takes on the appearance of Figure I.

Out of the hunger pole of the consuming theme comes the eating obsession of the novel, which leads to the initial revolt of the body and its rebellious return to natural processes. Birth and natural death both play their physical, organic roles[5] here, and still within the sphere of influence of the food theme: the fecund — but vegetating — Clara is also a member of a burial society, and Fish — at dinner, of course — expounds on the need for a new cataclysm, for the birth of the "goddess of birth and growth and death," the new Venus "big-bellied, teeming with life, potential, about to give birth to a new world in all its plenitude, a new Venus rising from the sea" (*EW*, p. 200). The ironic version of this damp Venus will prove to be Ainsley soaked in Len's baptismal beer. Fish will, understandably, adopt her, "patting her belly tenderly . . . his voice heavy with symbolic meaning" (*EW*, p. 241).

In order to sustain bodily life (which is, after all, a dynamic process), warmth is needed. And many of the narrative elements of the novel grouped around this pole are those involving either heat (for instance, Marian visits the pregnant Clara on a hot day and her body feels as if it is encased "in a layer of moist dough" [*EW*, p. 37]) or action — drowning, dissolving, drifting. What is interesting is that both of these clusters are viewed as negative at first, that is, from Marian's limited, unreliable point of view. It is, therefore, perceived as dangerous to be dissolving, drowning; the loss of a firm sense of identity by merging with the human or natural environment is a threat to Marian.[6] But the reader comes to see that these are necessary preludes to the salutary splitting of the restrictive seams (*EW*, p. 260) of that symbolic target-red dress that Peter liked so much, but which Marian correctly sensed to be alien from the start.

The other pole of love provides the organizing principle of all of the narrative themes[7] of possessing. Marriage is presented as owning, as consuming,[7] as

FIGURE 1

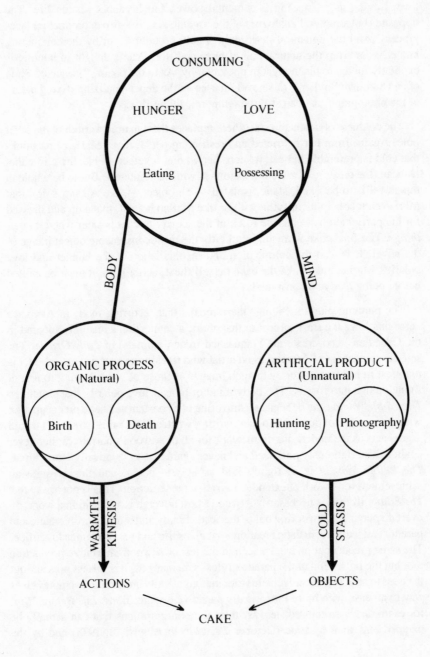

entrapment. The theme that was to be developed so fully in *Power Politics* is also present here as characters will and create their own traps, their own illusions in love. Loving as possessing is a mental power, but it cannot sustain life. The opposite (but structural analogue) of the organic here is artifice; product replaces process. And the unnatural death deliberately brought about by the conquering hunter is far from the natural end of birth and life. Peter's delight in hunting is explicitly linked to his interest in photography. As in the poem, "Projected Slide of an Unknown Soldier," this novel focuses on the depersonalizing, fixing nature of the photograph that can still the temporal, living flux.

The coldness of death and stasis here replaces the dynamic warmth of the other pole. Again, from her restricted and restricting perspective, Marian first thinks that cold is preferable to heat; it keeps her whole, together — like the girdle that Duncan (the creature of the cold) examines with such interest. But to be whole in this novel is to be fixed, static, isolated — an object — like Ainsley's doll that Marian cannot help identifying with or like Marian herself, made up and dressed for the party held by Peter, the Rock of the society that feels safer when it *owns things*. The final cake woman is explicitly the most consumable object image of the novel. It is also the culmination and reconciliation of the hunger and love polarity. Marian must bake the cake herself (heat, action), but it must be chilled before being *iced* and consumed.

The punning play on "icing" here recalls that recurring motif in Atwood's verse that links the stasis of ice[8] to that of art, a connection amusingly spoofed in the Canadian "con-create art" (squashed frozen animals) of *Lady Oracle*. The self-consciousness of Atwood as an artist who transforms process into product is manifest in her fascination with such images as those of water turning to ice, of living beings into fossils. The body/mind or hunger/love polarity that structures *The Edible Woman* can be seen as a mirroring of a constant aesthetic preoccupation with the paradox of process/product, writing/written. This same paradox, I would argue, acts as the underlying framework for all of Atwood's narratives, but never again is it so rigorously polarized and never again is it so "statically" structured. *The Edible Woman* is as tightly knit as a lyric poem, and this is quite an achievement for a work of extended narrative prose fiction. This is not to say that *The Edible Woman* is necessarily Atwood's best novel; it is a transitional work, an overt displaying and working out of the aesthetically and morally problematic and paradoxical nature of artistic creation — it gives life and yet condemns to artifice. The same preoccupation can be seen in the rest of Atwood's narrative production too, but the polarizing of the paradox is less schematized. It is no less present, but the need to structure the novelistic work metonymically around the two poles gives way to an ease with more intrinsically narrative organizations. *Life Before Man*, for example, is structured, less by thematic configurations that can actually be mapped out, than by time (October 29, 1976 to August 18, 1978) and by the dynamic, shifting psychological and moral changes that occur. The same is true of *Bodily Harm*.

By claiming a consistency of "preoccupation" in the novels, I do not mean to suggest that either the terms of the paradox or the exploratory images remain absolutely constant and unchanging. In *Surfacing*, for instance, the static photograph is replaced by the film, but the kinesis suggested by its "moving picture" is revealed to be only an illusion. "Random Samples" fixes, kills, and fragments. It too turns the living into the unnatural, the artificial. In this case, however, the victim is not an image, a metaphoric projection; it is a real person, that is, a character in the novel — Anna. Similarly, hunting ceases to be something talked about. Its victims litter the novel. And the photographer-father is a real (narrative) as well as symbolic force in the fiction. This move from the verbal metaphor to the narrative symbol is an important one in Atwood's development as a novelist. Here, for instance, *The Edible Woman's* technique of having characters with children, who also belong to a burial society, is replaced by a narrative event (a dive, almost a drowning) that produces a vision (real and imagined) which unites birth and death in a thematic continuum that proceeds to affect the narrative action of the surfaced heroine.

In *Surfacing*, the basic moral and aesthetic dualities of *The Edible Woman* persist, but their manifestation and function in the narrative begin to change. Theme and plot are integrated in a less rigorously schematic way, which suggests an increased ease with narrative form. But it might also mean that Atwood has perhaps discovered a supplementary way of exploring the aesthetic paradox that has allowed her to release part of the polarized tension that structured the first novel. The presence of an artist figure — the narrator is an illustrator — could be used to support this view, especially in the light of the next novel, *Lady Oracle*, in which the novelist heroine reconciles the process/product or life/art opposition, first, by her dual identity as Joan Foster/Delacourt, and then, by the increasing merging of her fantasy world of fiction and her lived world of experience. That *Lady Oracle* can also be read as an intertextual parody of Atwood's own preceding work[9] is not surprising, for this is but one other form of that same modernist (or "postmodernist") self-consciousness.

Like the later novel *Bodily Harm, Life Before Man* is, on the surface, a move away from this overt mode of self-reflectiveness. The creative power of the imagination is still a theme, but the context is that of life, not art. The distance between the aesthetic and the moral dimensions decreases. Lesje's learned but child-like fantasy world both compensates for and offers an escape from life, but it is a world that is left behind at the end of the novel, as life and real creativity — in the form of her as yet unborn child — assert themselves. The earlier pattern of images of stasis (ice, photograph) is replaced, or perhaps rather augmented, by a series of associations centred on the Royal Ontario Museum: fossils and bones of once very alive beasts, now reduced to fixed skeletal models, catalogued and labelled, safe from the disorder of real life. It is no wonder that Lesje finds a pregnant paleontologist a contradiction in terms (*LBM*, p. 308).

Sherrill Grace has argued that this novel, like *Two-Headed Poems*, represents a new stage in Atwood's development:[10] it is her first attempt at social and domestic realism unmediated by satire, comedy, or symbolism. While this is manifestly true on one level, *Life Before Man* is also very much a part of that same self-conscious preoccupation both with stasis — and the moral as well as artistic control that is implied in the creating of it — and also with the forces in society and in man that both fight and are defeated by this rage for order.

Society here teaches that safety and security lie in order, in control. Elizabeth's greatest fear is to be out of control, that is, to find herself dependent on others. The high price in moral and emotional terms that she must pay for her confining self-sufficiency is evident, both for herself and for Chris, whose fatal attraction to her was based on the fact that she had "what he wanted, power over a certain part of the world" (*LBM*, p. 161) and over himself. She is spiritually closer to her cold and unnatural Auntie Muriel than she can ever, consciously, face. Lesje too is caught in this circle game, but for her it is the labelling, the rational ordering of science that offers safety from the contingencies of life. Lacking Elizabeth's socialized power and control, Lesje turns to her cataloguing work and her science-inspired fantasies to create what is ultimately, as we shall see, "a known/land" (within the terms of *The Animals in That Country*). It is only at the end, when fantasy is denied and her job is threatened by her pregnancy, that the unknown natural order can assert itself. As Atwood writes in *You Are Happy*, "*this body is not reversible*" (*YAH*, p. 69). The mind, as in *The Edible Woman*, must be forced to listen to the body,[11] even if it means being fired from the R.O.M.

Atwood's choice of symbolic narrative locale for this novel does not come as a surprise to readers of her verse who recall the poem, "A Night in the Royal Ontario Museum" (also from *The Animals in That Country*). Here the R.O.M. is seen as a place to collect and label, a "crazed man-made/stone brain," "the mind's/deadend." Here life is fixed and dead. It is a "bone-/yard," where, as Lesje knows, entire "chunks of time lie . . . golden and frozen" (*LBM*, p. 308). But it is also safe compared to life outside, especially for the insecure and tentative Lesje. It is only at the end, when she can symbolically walk through the Gallery of Vertebrate Evolution in the wrong direction and sit there contemplating the foetus growing inside her, that Lesje fully perceives the fictional nature of the labels, the facts she has always turned to, both for solid support and also for material for her wish-fulfilling fantasies.[12]

The R.O.M. also functions as the focus of a theme that another poem (from the same collection) introduces. The poem is "Elegy for the Giant Tortoises," and the tortoises there are heading for extinction and museums, for a fate as "relics of what we have destroyed." Even if there were not a scene in the novel in which Lesje catalogues the remains of giant tortoises (*LBM*, p. 182), the title of the novel,

Life Before Man, would suggest to the reader the theme of extinction. There is an obvious and thematically important play on words here — life before man as the species and before man as the sex. Since the novel takes place in the present, in a life after dinosaurs, there is the suggestion that there could easily be a life *after* man — in the feminist and ecological sense as well (the latter being a fate that William, the environmental engineer, is always gloomily predicting). Like man, dinosaurs "didn't intend to become extinct; as far as they knew they would live forever" (*LBM*, p. 290).

That man shares this hubris is clear despite the dead bodies that litter this novel. Some of the dead are long in the past and therefore cannot be remembered: Nate's father who died in the War and Lesje's Aunt Rachel, a victim of the concentration camps. But people in this world take on the giant tortoise role of "relics of what we have destroyed," because, with the exception of Auntie Muriel's cancer, it is self-destruction that dominates. The novel opens a few weeks after Chris's bloody suicide. The effect of this act upon his rejecting lover, Elizabeth, is to stir up painful memories both of her catatonic sister Caroline, drowning in a bath, returning to the womb, and of her drunken mother, dead after a rooming house fire she started with her own cigarette. Every other female character in the novel contemplates or threatens suicide: Elizabeth (*LBM*, p. 301), Lesje (*LBM*, p. 293), Martha (*LBM*, p. 110). Even Nate's mother entered into her charity and political injustice campaigning as an alternative to suicide (*LBM*, p. 287), deciding to change, rather than exit from, a kind of world she knew she did not want to live in.

The first part of the novel ends on Hallowe'en, the eve of All Saints' Day. Waiting for costumed children to come to her door and still suffering from the shock of Chris's recent suicide, Elizabeth thinks: "They are souls, come back, crying at the door, hungry, mourning their lost lives. You give them food, money, anything to substitute for your love and blood, hoping it will be enough, waiting for them to go away" (*LBM*, p. 53). The next section opens on Remembrance Day. Still obsessed with memories of Chris, Elizabeth feels the pressure of the words of "In Flanders' Fields": "If ye break faith with us who die / We shall not sleep" (*LBM*, p. 57). Living in her memories, Elizabeth has no time for the present — but the present includes the 1976 election in Québec (*Je me souviens*) that Nate follows with great interest. This second part of the novel presents the R.O.M. as a kind of cemetery of the past where even the model of a paleontologist in a display case seems to Lesje to look like a corpse. The planetarium next door, which Elizabeth visits, is a graveyard of the future, of cosmic disasters, black holes. In the present, Elizabeth has only memories of personal disasters, particularly of Chris's and Caroline's deaths. Nate, on the other hand, has to face Martha's fake suicide, a gesture that ironically echoes Caroline's first fake suicide which symbolized her catatonic regression and her decision to leave her body behind (*LBM*, p. 181).

Seeking oblivion *in* her body, Elizabeth turns to the safe, the cliché, the panty salesman she met on the subway. All she wants is "A termination. *Terminal*," we are told (*LBM*, p. 226). A few pages later this last word comes back to haunt the novel. In one of his two flashbacks, Nate remarks (when Elizabeth leaves Chris but he persists in returning) that her "way of disposing of her lovers was usually terminal," a rather heavy irony given Chris's subsequent suicide. However, as Chris's death recedes into the past of the novel and into the past of Elizabeth's somewhat revisionist memory, the death theme alters. Auntie Muriel (of whom it had earlier been stated that she could not "be said to live") actually dies of cancer. Elizabeth's blackout at her grave seems to signal an unconscious identification with and perhaps a subsequent rebirth of the woman and values she professed to hate. The death/birth conjunction is clear here, as in *The Edible Woman, Surfacing*, and even *Lady Oracle* (with its fake drowning and secret resurrection). It is perhaps most emphatic at the end of *Life Before Man*. In anger and out of the "fear of being nothing," Lesje thinks of suicide, momentarily identifying with Chris (*LBM*, p. 293), but instead she throws out her birth control pills and opts for life — albeit a vengeful one.[13]

This death-obsessed novel begins after a suicide and ends before a birth; however, under the golden dome of the R.O.M. where Lesje, Elizabeth, and Chris all worked, neither of the two poles in *The Edible Woman* appears to dominate thematically in the deaths of people and relationships. Out of revenge, threatened death, anger, and failing relationships, comes the promise, at least, of new life.[14] Creation can and does assert itself, but not in artistic form. There is no Joan Foster in this novel. Nate does make rocking horses and other toys, but he sees these first as regressions and by the end only as museum pieces of his past. Chris has built taxidermic animal models at the R.O.M. But any artistic pretensions to their work would appear to be undercut by Atwood in the parodic presence of the girl at Martha's party who makes plastic models of Holstein cows for breeders and dealers but hopes to get into "painted portraits of individual cows, for which she could get more money" (*LBM*, p. 108). Atwood had embedded a similar parody in *The Edible Woman* in the Lawrentian Fish's praise of birth: "the very process of artistic creation was itself an imitation of Nature, of the thing in nature that was most important to the survival of Mankind" (*EW*, p. 198). Because he sees the artist as "pregnant with his work," his taking on of Ainsley and her forthcoming child is credible: graduate students and academics have a role in caring for the creative.

In the first novel, this important notion of creativity is explicitly thematized, discussed overtly as in an essay. By the time Atwood wrote *Life Before Man* it had been more fully integrated into the narrative structures themselves, and *Bodily Harm* is the product of this integration. The increased ease with the constraints (and liberties) of the novel form is also to be seen in Atwood's use of point of view. In *The Edible Woman*, the change in the narrative voice from first-person to third, and then back to first, explicitly (*EW*, p. 278) reflects the psychological changes of the heroine. The binary vision of opposites that structures Atwood's lyric poems reappears in Marian's two principles of identity. The cool, distanced first-person voice of *Surfacing* is not unlike the somewhat sardonic, retrospectively ironic one of *Lady Oracle* since in both cases the self-alienation of the narrator and, therefore, the unreliability of her point of view are signalled to the reader by the discrepancy between narrative tone and actual event.

In *Life Before Man*, Atwood turns again to the third-person centre-of-consciousness technique of the middle part of *The Edible Woman*, but here she chooses three characters, Nate being the first male to be granted such a position in her fiction. Only Elizabeth is allowed a few, brief, first-person segments to give voice and immediacy to her anguish over Chris's suicide. The prevailing tense of narration is the present and most sections begin with a physical situating of the character whose perspective will be presented: "Elizabeth sits" is perhaps the most frequent.[15] There are only two flashbacks, both Nate's and both involving Elizabeth and Chris. In the first, Chris is the victor; in the second (just before his suicide), he is the victim. The rest of the novel is structured by the rigid chronology of specific dates. Unlike *The Edible Woman* but like *Bodily Harm* later, *Life Before Man* provides a very strong sense of time and of psychological development through time; static image patterns are replaced by equally carefully structured but definitely temporal strategies.

The number of sections devoted to each of the three perspectives in any one part is never random. The logic that determines the distribution is a temporal and narrative one. For instance, part one takes place over only three days, and the three characters all have a section on each day, but Nate and Elizabeth get an added one at the end, on Hallowe'en. Elizabeth is, after all, trying to come to terms with Chris's death, and Nate is finishing off one relationship and trying to begin another. Lesje, however, does not really figure yet in either of their lives, or in the novel's action; she is merely bored with William but unwilling to do anything about it. The second part covers a longer time span (November 12–December 28, 1976), and the only day given from all three perspectives is the important one that sees Lesje take Nate and his children on a tour of the R.O.M. while Elizabeth visits the planetarium. The Nate/Lesje situation and the later problematic relationship with the children is here presented in foreshadowing microcosm. Elizabeth is absent, but just next door.

The only triple-viewed scene in part three is Elizabeth's disastrous dinner party at which are displayed the fears of all three characters regarding the threatening developing relationship between Nate and Lesje. In this part of the novel Nate has fewer sections, and this reduction of his narrative reflects his absence from action. It is at this point that Elizabeth begins the manipulations that will end in William's quasi-rape of Lesje and in Lesje's move which will, ironically, set up the scene for Nate's leaving (the scene that provides the only tri-vision sections in part four). Nate's first flashback to the chess game in Chris's room, where Elizabeth's infidelity is made insultingly clear, follows significantly on his love-making with Lesje — in Elizabeth's bed. The last part of the novel begins with the three characters' views of the divorce negotiation visit and ends on a day whose events reflect the consequences of that visit. Nate (in two sections) is reconciled to Elizabeth — as part of his past — and to his mother, that is, to himself as very much her son. He is also open to whatever the immediate future with Lesje might bring. Lesje overcomes her past fear of Elizabeth, renounces her fantasy world, and moves into the present and the real. Elizabeth, who had begun the novel, ends it, alone, firmly rooted in a less than perfect reality, longing for an ideal, communal, secure world, here symbolized by the propagandistic Chinese peasant art. The last words of the novel are: "China does not exist. Nevertheless she longs to be there." This careful psychological and temporal structuring of *Life Before Man* is far from rigid. It is not obtrusive, but functions within the confines of the novel genre's conventions. For example, Nate's sections follow and respond to those of one of his women — until the moment in part four when he sees himself as "segmented man," "a tin man, his heart stuffed with sawdust" (*LBM*, p. 246). This moment of self-revelation, which has been prepared for in the novel, does not however change Nate for long. True, his section begins part five, but Lesje and Elizabeth soon take the controlling roles in the narrative and in forming Nate's future. His last section in the book narratively and verbally echoes his last one in part one. Perhaps, it is implied, nothing has changed from October 31, 1976 to August 18, 1978. The temporal and the psychological, the formal and the moral, cannot be separated in this novel, or perhaps in any traditional narrative literary form.

The Edible Woman's static thematic configurations are more closely related to the structural identity of the lyrics, with their binary focus. But the later novels show yet another change away from verse structures toward more narrative forms: a comparison of *The Edible Woman* with *Life Before Man* reveals that the secondary, that is, fantasy worlds are presented differently in the two novels. Earlier we saw that the level of textual self-consciousness about the moral and aesthetic dimensions of creative process alters in explicitness from the clear static/ dynamic polarity in the first novel (and, significantly, also in the poetry) to the "narrativization" of these tensions between product and process in the plot of *Surfacing*, to the use of overt artist figures in *Lady Oracle*. The highly imaginative heroines of all of these novels indulge in fantasies whose creative processes often seem to function as mirrors of the novelist's own act. In these works the change in reference level, from the objective world of fact (fictive fact, of course) to the fantasy world of the mind, is signalled in a variety of ways. This can be accomplished by a subtle change in linguistic register, to relative verbal extrava- gance or deviations from the text's tonal norm that mark the presence of symbolic dimensions, as in *Surfacing*, or, as in *The Edible Woman*, on a more overt level, by Marian's conscious identification with the food she is about to consume, or by

Duncan's bald statement that he and Marian have symbiotic fantasy lives (*EW*, p. 264). Whatever the device used, or the level of explicitness, in each case there is a referential shift from the world of (novelistic) reality to that of the subjective, private reality of the characters' psyches. This is not surprising, given that the novels are all, in some way, novels about identity and perception.

To point to the intrapsychic nature of the reference, Atwood applies the lessons Freud taught about the symbolic properties of the unconscious. The regressive and wish-fulfilling fantasies of the characters are often presented in highly metaphoric and associative terms. By *Life Before Man*, however, Atwood has extended this psychic referential level to other than clear fantasy worlds. For example, the attempts of the characters to cope with traumatic psychological blows are reflected in the language and structure of the novel itself. Chris's suicide is the focus for Elizabeth of a network of associations about sex, death, and power. The associations in part one are immediate, strong, and purely verbal. Wanting to protect herself from Chris's power over her, even in memory, she gives us the clue to that power in her play on armadillo and armored dildo (*LBM*, p. 11). The play on "Sultry. Sultan. Sullen" (*LBM*, p. 23) sums up Chris's spirit and fate, as does the chain of associations around his eyes that glint "like nailheads. Copperheads. Pennies on the eyes" (*LBM*, p. 24). By part two the associations move to the narrative level, more removed from the verbal immediacy, as the death becomes distanced from (and worked out in) Elizabeth's own unconscious. Remembrance Day conjures up the need to keep faith with the dead. The planetarium show leaves Elizabeth upset yet sure that people "do not become stars of any kind when they die" (*LBM*, p. 78). A child's book of riddles has one about a coffin: Elizabeth reads it while in a bathtub full of "Bodykins" bubble bath bought for Chris.[16] But as Elizabeth comes to re-interpret (and repress) Chris's death — as something he did to *her* — her obsession and guilt (which Nate's second flashback helps us to understand) are dissipated, or are displaced, and so too are the verbal and narrative associations. Back in control, Elizabeth notices that time has not stood still "while she's been away" (*LBM*, p. 139), that is, away from reality, living in her own psychic world.

It is only in part four, with Nate gone and her control again slipping, that the verbal play returns. The word play describing Elizabeth's desire for oblivion in casual sex ("A termination. *Terminal.*") points back to Chris's death and her psychic state at that time. She sees herself: "Stewed, descending the staircase" (*LBM*, p. 248), her smile locked into place, "*Lockjaw.*" When her daughter asks about Elizabeth's future death, the following widely linking verbal network is set up: "*Mummy*. A dried corpse in a guilded case. *Mum*, silent. *Mama*, short for mammary gland" (*LBM*, p. 250). The novel's moral themes about human relationships as they exist in time all seem to be summed up in this passage, a passage which is also a convincing example of psychological realism.[17]

Atwood once said of her early fiction: "To a large extent the characters are creating the world which they inhabit, and I think we all do that to a certain extent, or we certainly do a lot of rearranging,"[18] In all of her novels, however, characters also create worlds which *only* they can inhabit, private fantasy worlds of daydream that offer escape from and consolation for the world which they must inhabit but cannot alter beyond a certain point. Atwood's interest in this kind of second order novelistic reference is likely, as suggested earlier, another manifestation of her self-consciousness about the creative process. It was Freud once again who pointed to the links in motivation between the creative imagination and daydreaming.[19] In some of Atwood's novels, temporary fantasies are presented as salutary and indeed necessary to the psychic health and peace of the character (*Surfacing*). But in others, these substitute worlds are seen as escapes, as wish-fulfilling improvements, that actually inhibit coming to terms with reality and with other people. When the flamboyant Royal Porcupine turns into plain old Chuck Brewer in *Lady Oracle*, Joan is disappointed: "For him, reality and fantasy were the same thing, which meant that for him there was no reality. But for me it would mean there was no fantasy, and therefore no escape" (*LO*, p. 270).

In *Life Before Man*, Lesje has a similar regressive need to escape, this time from the boring or threatening present to a prehistorical world of her own making. This extension of her childhood book-inspired day-dreams thematically links life before man (prehistory) to life before men. The qualities of her fantasy that are revealing are its imaginative violation of the "official version of paleontological reality" (*LBM*, p. 18) and Lesje's role in it as that of "blissful, uninvolved," distanced observer. "Lesje" is translated as "Alice," and, as a young girl, her wonderland is explicitly linked to the world of novelistic creation: when she discovers her lush, tropical new land, "crawling with wondrous life forms, all of them either archaic and thought extinct, or totally unknown even in fossil records," she will name it Lesjeland. Of course, Lesjeland already exists in her imagination, for as a child she could even make "careful drawings of this land in her scrapbooks" and label all the flora and fauna (*LBM*, p. 92).

Contact with Lesje appears to inspire Nate with similar, but this time adolescent, regressive fantasies which he directly links to masturbatory memories of a matinee performance of *She*: holding Lesje "would be like holding some strange plant, smooth, thin, with sudden orange flowers. *Exotics*, the florist called them. The light would be odd, the ground underfoot littered with bones" (*LBM*, p. 71). Lesje, like the Royal Porcupine, must remain a mystery (*LBM*, 72). The blatant adolescent wish-fulfilling quality of his other fantasies is equally evident. For example, he tries to wish away the torturing Elizabeth by turning her into various undignified substances, like vanilla pudding, just as he used to metamorphose his teachers in school.

Lesje and Nate are also both victims of each other's imaginations, an example of the serious implications of a situation, like Marian and Duncan's, of complementary fantasies. Lesje is "addicted to Nate's version of her," she claims; she wants so much to be the ideal serene refuge image that Nate has created of her (*LBM*, p. 267), instead of being someone who, in clothing stores, looks "for something that might become her, something she might become" (*LBM*, p. 26). Nate too finds his beard shaved off one day: "His hands have decided it's time for him to be someone else" (*LBM*, p. 43). He goes to Lesje because she, unlike Elizabeth, takes him seriously and also because he is attracted to her remoteness, her distance. She is "unattainable, shining like the crescent moon" (*LBM*, p. 130). To go to Lesje would be to leap "in mid-air, hurtled into a future he could not yet imagine" but which seems increasingly preferable to staying with Elizabeth "on the solid earth . . . feet on the ground" (*LMB*, p. 163). Later in the novel, he does try to jump for "that nonexistent spot where he longs to be. Mid-air" (*LBM*, 288), between the moon and the ground, uncommitted, free or (as the immediately preceding fantasy projection has it), "Motherless, childless . . . the solitary wanderer" (*LBM*, p. 287).

While it is true that boredom, embarrassment and frustations can be momentarily evaded through fantasy, such escapes are not permanent. Reality intrudes: "Lesje is in the living room, in the Upper Jurassic." In her fantasy she tries to run, but the thumping of her binoculars bothers her: "There's nowhere else she wants to be, but this time it isn't exploration; she knows the terrain too well. It's merely flight" (*LBM*, p. 264). Fantasy worlds like this are not unknown worlds; they are created, fixed ones. They may try to recreate life, as Lesje's imagination had always tried to make the dinosaur bones flesh out and live again, but the main motivation was to permit her to "move among the foliage . . . an expedition of one" (*LBM*, p. 310). At the end of the novel, with an unknown world before her (a possible pregnancy, a shaky relationship with Nate), Lesje renounces fantasy: "But she can't do it. Either she's lost faith or she's too tired" (*LBM*, p. 311). She is no longer like Nate's children, dressing up in their mother's or grandmother's clothes; she has grown up and must accept the responsibility for her own life, a life she has created by choice.

Like the narrator of *Surfacing* earlier and *Bodily Harm* later, she finally renounces the passivity that permits victimization and opts for life and responsibility. The truly creative act of her pregnancy becomes the real paradigm of the novelist's act of creation, an act of moral responsibility for the creation of life. As in *Surfacing* and *Bodily Harm* once again, distance disappears when the observer takes responsibility for and accepts the world he or she creates and inhabits. Rather than signalling a change in Atwood's work, *Life Before Man* is the culmination of her integration of the moral and aesthetic dimensions within the context of that modern narrative self-consciousness that, while directing the reader's attention to the fictive nature of the world of the novel, will nevertheless *not* allow him to evade its moral implications. The reader of Atwood's novels can never be passive; he must accept responsibility for the world he too is bringing to life by his act of reading.[20] The answer to the static "carven word" is the reading process that mirrors the dynamic creative act of the writer.

Notes

1. James Sloan Allan, "Self-Consciousness and the Modernist Temper," *Georgia Review* 33 (1979): 601–20.
2. Frank Davey, "Atwood's Gorgon Touch," *Studies in Canadian Literature* 2 (1977): 146–63; Rosemary Sullivan, "Breaking the Circle," *Malahat Review* 41 (1977) 30–41; Sherrill Grace, *Violent Duality* (Montréal: Véhicule Press, 1980).
3. "The Symbolic Cannibals," *Canadian Literature* 42 (1969): 98–100.
4. This circling schematization of metonymic contiguity as inclusion is a version of that proposed by the Groupe *Mu* of Liège in their *Rhétorique générale* (Paris: Larousse, 1970), p. 117.
5. This is also true in the story, "Giving Birth" (*DG*, especially, p. 249) where the title itself also suggests that birth, like death, is an event, not a thing. It is a process, not a product, and for this reason, all the more difficult to express in static words.
6. At the office party she feels herself submerged in a "thick sargasso-sea of femininity": "she was one of them, her body the same, identical, merged with that other flesh" (*EW*, p. 167). Afterwards she flees to the cold park. In the bathtub, preparing for Peter's party, "she was afraid that she was dissolving, coming apart layer by layer" (*EW*, P. 218). She quickly gets out of the tub, feeling "safer" on the cold tiled floor.
7. The connection is made in an amusing juxtaposition of connotations in the scene in which Marian walks "slowly down the aisle, keeping pace with the gentle music" — but the aisle is not of a church, but of a supermarket (*EW*, p. 172).
8. See Sherrill Grace's extended discussion of this theme in *Violent Duality*, pp. 10, 51–52, 65–67, 77.
9. Ibid., pp. 111–28.
10. Ibid., p. 135.
11. Marian cuts her cake doll at the neck, where head joins body. See also *Sfg*, p. 121: "At some point my neck must have closed over, pond freezing or a wound, shutting me into my head."
12. Just before this Lesje has the urge to cry out to those who want, as she did, definitions and facts in science: "*The Mesozoic isn't real. It's only a word for a place you can't go to any more because it isn't there. It's called the Mesozoic because we call it that*" (*LBM*, p. 290).
13. A child born of revenge, Lesje fears, is sure to be a mutant or a reptile (*LBM*, p. 293), an image that is echoed in Elizabeth's description of her dead aunt as an old reptile (*LBM*, p. 297). The birth/death metaphors here and elsewhere act as underlying sources of connections between otherwise disparate sections.
14. Though the male/female relationships do not fare well, each of the main characters establishes an important interrelation with a figure of his or her past in the last part of the novel. Nate sees at last how similar he is to his mother in her despair; Elizabeth really is Auntie Muriel's niece and adopted daughter in more ways than the legal; Lesje comes to value her similarities to her two very different grandmothers.
15. Elizabeth's bitter parody of "In Flanders' Fields" may hold the key to the predominance of this recurrent opening pose: "We are the numb. Long years ago/We did this or that. And now we sit" (*LBM*, p. 100).
16. The constant stress on Chris's "salt body," "dense as earth," reinforces his sexual power and danger for Elizabeth and makes his particular choice of mode of suicide understandable. As Nate perceives: "Chris's expression had never really been in that heavy flat face of his . . . It had been in his body. The head had been a troublemaker, which was probably why Chris had chosen to shoot at it" (*LBM*, p. 16).

17. When upset, Nate too is presented as making these verbal associations: "He had been separated; he is separate. Dismembered. He is no longer a member" (*LBM*, p. 244).
18. In an interview with G. Gibson in *Eleven Canadian Novelists* (Toronto: Anansi, 1973), p. 23.
19. "Creative Writers and Daydreaming," in *The Standard Edition of the Complete Psychological Works of Sigmund Freud*, ed. James Strachey (London: Hogarth Press and the Institute of Psycho-Analysis, 1953–1974), 9: 143–53.
20. For a very full examination of the developing stages in the activity of reading, see the work of Wolfgang Iser, especially *The Implied Reader* (Baltimore: Johns Hopkins University Press, 1974) and *The Act of Reading* (Baltimore: Johns Hopkins University Press, 1978).

3

The Pronunciation of Flesh:
A Feminist Reading of Margaret Atwood's Poetry

Barbara Blakely

The poetry of Margaret Atwood pivots round the circle game,[1] round the struggle to name and transforms this game. This "round cage of glass" (*CG*, p. 44) is the game of power, the imperialism of eye, word and touch, the game of enclosure by representation. Its closed rules define the entire field of existence.

However, the central paradigm of the game is sexual. "I" — woman — and "you" — man — are the subjects of this game, builders and inhabitants of the enclosure. Man and woman do not exist separately, as independent beings, but only "arm in arm, neither/joined nor separate" (*CG*, p. 43), the only point being to go round and round. They mutually construct and define each other's identities and, conversely, constrain and limit each other. The very being of one is founded by the operations of the other. These are operations of touch:

> I touch you, I am created in you
> somewhere as a complex
> filament of light.
>
> (*AC*, p. 64)

> My hands
> where they touch you, create
> small inhabited islands
>
> (*AC*, p. 69)

They are also operations of the eye, where one gives or commands the reflection of the other. Both are trapped in the infinite regress of mirrors:

> You refuse to be
> (and I)
> an exact reflection, yet
> will not walk from the glass,
> be separate.
>
> (*CG*, p. 36)

And they are operations of speech; each longs for words that will give expression to the desired life:

> . . . mouth against mouth,
> lips moving in these desperate
> attempts at speech,
> rescuer bending over the drowned body
> trying to put back the breath, the soul.

(*YAH*, p. 10)

It is the entire known world they construct as they fashion each other.

In an examination of these operations which construct a world, where man and woman create and engage each other in the circle game, the phenomenological perspective of Maurice Merleau-Ponty offers a paradigm which a feminist reading may call upon.[2] Within this paradigm, the meaning of the world, and our human identities as woman and man, are not givens but are the products of our consciousness and our interactions.

There is no definition of existence, no human identity, apart from the world that is constructed through human consciousness, given shape and meaning through language, perception, and action. We are present first in this world as flesh; this given existence is not yet meaningful. Only in moving, touching, acting, desiring do we claim this existence as our own. Only thus do we make this world visible to our perceptions by choosing our perspective within it. From this source of flesh and perception, speech arises, words giving traces of corporeal intentions, expressions of carnal perceptions. Language ultimately creates significance in a world which exists before and around us, yet is not ours until it is articulated. Through these operations of the body (touch, gesture, posture), of the eye (image and reflection), and speech, human existence is constituted and given meaning.

And through these operations self and other meet and constitute each other, becoming subject, not object. Woman and man exist not absolutely, but only as axes in a relationship, defining the field of existence. As poles creating and created by a common field, they are both dependent upon, yet differentiated from, each other. They exist separately only by existing together, by jointly articulating time and space in the operations of body, eye, and speech. They create themselves by viscerally embodying the images projected by the other, by mirroring and exchanging views, and by determining stories which assign oppositional roles: "At first I was given centuries / to wait in caves" for you who "would never come back," you who "jangled off / into the mountains." The script shifts, but the subjects' functions remain the same (*PP*, pp. 28–29).

Identity is given through "ancient habit," "this net" of "nose against neck, knee thrown / over the soft groin," where each is "half of a pair, / half of a custom" (*THP*, p. 21). Man and woman, whose voices speak antiphonally, are signs in a language of sexual intersubjectivity[3] requiring and answering each other:

[handwritten margin note: • the world is not ours; we are merely a part of the ultimate reality]

He said: the end of walls, the end of ropes, the opening
of doors, a field, the wind, a house, the sun, a table,
an apple.

She said: nipple, arms, lips, wine, belly, hair, bread,
thighs, eyes, eyes.
[. . .]

He said: foot, boot, order, city, fist, roads, time,
knife.

She said: water, night, willow, rope hair, earth belly,
cave, meat, shroud, open, blood.

(*THP*, pp. 50–51)

Although we exist as objects before and apart from each other, we require this
engagement with the other to become subject, to attain identity. We are necessarily
mirrored, held by the other's touch, sight and word; therefore each suffers the
inevitable distortions of perceptual gaps between visible surfaces and the private
interior, between the seen and the seer, between the activity of naming and the
passivity of being named.[4] In the inevitable narcissism of world construction, it is
the world as well as the self that the subject constructs in her own image. At the
same time, she is implicated in the world construction of the other:

I exist in two places,
        here and where you are.

Pray for me
not as I am but as I am.

(*YAH*, p. 44)

Each is vulnerable to introjection and consummation by the other:

More and more frequently the edges
of me dissolve and I become
a wish to assimilate the world, including
you, if possible through the skin. . . .

(*AC*, p. 53)

Each surrenders to the projections of images by the other upon the self:

You refuse to own
yourself, you permit
others to do it for you:

> you become slowly more public,
> in a year there will be nothing left
> of you but a megaphone . . . .

(PP, p. 30)

They are subject to a confusion of body images and boundaries, where

> . . . we hurtle towards each other
> at the speed of sound, everything roars
>
> we collide sightlessly and
> fall, the pieces of us
> mixed as disaster . . . .

(PP, p. 11)

Similarly, they refuse to recognize authorship of the construction: "Whose house is this / we both live in / but neither of us owns" (*PP*, p. 48), and are unable to take responsibility for what is expressed and to read what is communicated:

> . . . you have gone, your last
> message to me left
> illegible on the mountain
> road, quick
> scribble of glass and blood . . . .

(PP, p. 18)

This is the circle game.

In Atwood's circle game of sexual intersubjectivity, these misconceptions are neither benign nor inevitable. The contours of the field of relationships are governed by power politics, an essentially violent sexual politics.[5] The dynamics of this game determine the operations of speaking, seeing, and acting, and through the medium of the word comes dismemberment of the body:

> with this cleaver of a pencil
> I hack off your aureole.
>
> I can make you armless, legless;

(AC, p. 60)

as well as the obliteration of the seeing (mirroring) eye:

> I deny
> your goldrimmed visions
> by scratching through your eyes.
>
> *(AC*, p. 60)

Though Atwood's game is a mutual construction, dominance of the field belongs finally to man, "the hugest monster" (*PU*, p. 43), in whom violence is a determinative characteristic: "the ends of your fingers bleed / from 1000 murders" (*PP*, p. 47). Negation is his way of life as he consumes and abolishes even the generative energy of the sun. Possessive and oppressive, "whistling and destructive, and / carefree as a hurricane" (*AC*, p. 60), man determines woman's universe, measures and fixes the topography of her being. This "memorizer / of names (to hold / these places / in their proper places)" (*CG*, p. 39) possesses woman further by "word-/ plays," by "calculated ploys / of the body, the witticisms / of touch" (*CG*, p. 39). These operations refuse her initiative, her autonomy, and eventually deny her existence entirely. He fixes her in the field of his own "mind's continent"; her contours are traced by eye "like a country's boundary." She is

> transfixed
> by your eyes'
> cold blue thumbtacks.
>
> *(CG*, p. 40)

In the definition of oppression discussed by Paolo Freiere,[6] one group oppresses another when the first group names and determines the other's existence, allowing the second group no power to define its existence for itself. In Atwood's circle game, man oppresses woman through the operations of eye, body, and word so completely that she is trapped in the circle of his consciousness, unable to name herself or to name him. Further, Atwood suggests that man's refusal of woman's being provides the paradigm for other oppressions, other violence, and that the destructive use of power is most often sexual at its core:

> You'll notice that what they have in common
> is between the legs. Is this
> why wars are fought?
> Enemy territory, no man's
> land, to be entered furtively . . . .
>
> *(TS*, p. 55)

Woman is subsumed within man's paradigm of existence for his purposes of self and world construction, to inhabit his mind's continent and to be grasped as his perfect mirroring lover.

To designate this a "feminist reading" of Margaret Atwood's poetry is not to designate her a feminist nor her work a feminist programme. It is not, further, to search her work for evidences of those "fashionable minority psychologies" located there by John Wilson Foster,[7] nor to applaud her for her "cultural or civic consciousness" as does Rosemary Sullivan.[8] It is to suggest that the condition of possibility[9] of her writing and of this reading is the critical consciousness of sexual politics made explicit in feminist theory. It is to see dominant within her work paradigms of woman and man, their identity, interaction and mutual construction. It is to see, with Atwood, the circle game as a field of sexual politics and to recognize her disclosure of the politics of sight, touch, and speech. She delineates the means by which woman and man are present to each other in sexual relationship, through the operations of perception, action and expression; she demonstrates how these operations are vulnerable to control by a consciousness intending not mutuality but oppression. Her poetry is moved by the drive toward transcendence of the sexual circle game, through description of its contours, through projection of alternate consciousness, and through transformation of eye, body, and word. Atwood's exploration of the world of woman and man can thus be read through a feminist paradigm of oppression and transformation, within a phenomenological model of sexual intersubjectivity.

In the transformation of the circle game, the contours of the game must first be delineated and the means of oppression detailed. The eye is the first of these instruments. Man's eye is governed by the masculine intentionality of domination. It becomes an instrument of control and freezes the flux of relationship with woman. His eye can "petrify reflection;" in his gaze woman sees herself "turn frigid as your sad / mirror" (*AC*, p. 25). Woman's eye, on the other hand, is vulnerable to attack — "a fish hook / an open eye" — vulnerable to possession by man. Using his own eye as instrument of capture, he seizes her power of reflection and constitutes her as mirror in his self-construction:

> fall into me,
>
> it will be your own
> mouth you hit, firm and glassy,
>
> your own eyes you find you
> are up against   closed   closed.

> (*YAH*, p. 24)

She gives him himself, preserves him, and keeps him safe by making of herself a perfect surface.[10] She is passive, expressionless, "breath withheld, no anger / or joy disturbing the surface" (*YAH*, p. 26).

Similarly, she weaves for him a mirage: "I spin you a night and you hide in it" (*PP*, p. 43); she assembles for him a collage history: "an object, a watch, a picture / you claim as yours" (*PP*, p. 26). She is reduced to a mirror — "life of vision only"(*YAH*, p. 27), but it is not her own world she reflects. She serves as the focal point of man's world and his position within it.

Water is a possible instrument of reflection, where "that other self of mine" also kneels on the rock, gathering berries "in either world" (*PU*, p. 8). It becomes instead a distorting medium, where there are "diffuse / surfaces, angles of refraction" and "the obsolescence of vistas" (*PU*, p. 23). It is the environment of the drowned from "This is a photograph of me," of those obliterated from history, who cannot be seen clearly. While woman is blurred — "the effect of water / on light is a distortion" (*CG*, p. 11) — man is deceptively doubled in a monstrous reflection of the "fierce god/head crested with blue flame" (*PU*, p. 9) who elsewhere "would not let himself be seen" (*AC*, p. 24).

Sight thus governed by the politics of dominance is not free for the mutual constitution of self and other. There can be no play of expression and gesture in which each discovers the other in the self and creates the self in the other in a necessary chiasmus of points of view.[11] Instead, man captures woman in celluloid mimesis, in a series of still shots, in the composition of the "organized instant" (*CG*, p. 45). Intimate knowledge is shunned in favour of plastic poses, compensated for by adopting the borrowed postures of a "bad movie," speaking and moving "through an air stale with aphorisms" (*PP*, p. 3), and settling for the mime of happy heterosexuality, "the mirage of us / hands locked, smiling" (*PP*, p. 23).

In a series of poses pretending contentment, man and woman play out public roles and caricature male and female stereotypes such as the *pietà*, the Madonna cradling the body of Christ (*PP*, p. 6). Man and woman are then bound to these paradigms, which become a closed room of mute perceptions: "the doors are shut, you aren't talking" and "I do nothing" (*PP*, p. 44). Each sees the other through the perceptual grid of desire and demand, holding the other on the focal point of need so that sight does not open the eye to create the world in its light but sets up points for attack, or circles for target practice.

The second operation, touch, is again dominated by imperialist intentions. Flesh is not the fluid medium of delight but the reification of violence or its colonized victim. Man's touch assures him ownership of woman's universe and his right to set its elements in proper relation to himself:

> you touch my head
> the splintered
> universe and

> look, how the moon
> and sun rise, arc across and set
> once more above you properly
>
> (*AC*, p. 57)

To this end, man cauterizes his flesh, his senses, turning himself into an "impervious glass tower" (*PP*, p. 32). Woman is the object shaped by his hands at their will. She is "turned to crystal," broken open by the vacuum of his "empty hands" (*PP*, p. 42), or stroked by them to become "like the moon / seen from the earth" (*THP*, p. 11). He seizes her bodily, incorporating her into his self-constructions, into his "heroic / struggle to become real" (*PP*, p. 7).

Because reified flesh cannot serve as the medium of communion, of extension into the world of the other or reception of the other's offerings,[12] man's flesh becomes an obstacle, hardened and impervious. He is monstrous, a robot mechanism with a face that "unhinges and comes apart" (*YAH*, p. 88). He refuses sensual touch: "you clench yourself, withhold / even your flesh / outline" (*PP*, p. 34); he rejects the vulnerability of receiving pleasure when it is offered and retains control: "pleasure is what / you take but will not accept" (*PP*, p. 34). His body is no longer animated and animating but mute and inert, not the disclosure of desires and feelings but the embodiment of deception.

Woman, on the other hand, is vulnerable, unable to protect the boundaries of her self and body. She is subject to dismemberment and to invasion and colonization: "you twisted your own wide spaces / and made them include me" (*CG*, p. 69). The geometry of her world is pulled into conformity with his, as he disassembles and reconstructs it:

> You collapse my house of cards
> merely by breathing
>
> . . .
>
> and put together my own
> body, another
>
> place
>
> for me to live
> in.
>
> (*CG*, p. 71)

The central purpose of this colonization and dismemberment is sexual control. Woman is "no man's / land, to be entered furtively, / fenced, owned but never surely, / scene of these desperate forays" (*TS*, p. 55). She must be put together as the body which man would like her to be so that his sexual authority is assured.

Man similarly fences the land, imposes the order of the "trail of single reason" on a landscape "where geometries are multiple" (*AC*, 4). Furthermore, the horizon he rides toward is understood as woman, the locus of his existence, and the *prima materia* of his life. In a paradoxical metaphor of birth, he moves into and through her, clutching at life, perceiving her as both the "outside" and the medium he must wrench his way through to freedom. At the same time he must destroy the power of woman because she has given him flesh: like the woman in "Christmas Carols," her child is violently extracted and "she was thrown away, / useless, a ripped sack" (*TS*, p. 56). Nor can woman's power to create through her own flesh be used at her own will. There again she will be subject to invasion and colonization, "thirty / times raped & pregnant by the enemy" (*TS*, p. 56).

Birth in the masculine metaphor is the gesture of Frankenstein/Adam splitting the rib from his side: "it is a living / skeleton, mine, round, / that lies on the plate before me" (*AC*, p. 42), bastard flesh of an asexual creation, "secret / form of the heart . . . . Blood of my brain" (*AC*, pp. 43-45). Through de-composing and re-membering his own flesh, man, claiming woman's mythological role as "universal weaver," creates "with delicate precision" a creature in his own image and reflection. The "destroyed god" which results is the perfection of man, but this "rubble of tendons, / knuckles and raw sinews" (*AC*, p. 44) is already rotting. Man's own violence is cut loose, incarnated and reified, and turns to destroy its creator, its twin.

On the other hand, woman, here Susanna Moodie, wishes to retain faith in creation through flesh and touch:

> the hands produce objects   the world touched
> into existence: was
> this cup, this village here
> before my fingers
>
> (*JSM*, p. 52)

She has been unable to maintain the visceral structures of her former world: "My heirloom face I brought / with me a crushed eggshell / among other debris" (*JSM*, p. 24). She therefore incarnates a new relationship with her world: "I grew a chapped tarpaulin / skin; I negotiated the drizzle / of strange meaning" (*JSM*, p. 15). Although she worked "all those years" as one of the settlers, "building up this edifice / . . . this crumbling hovel" (*JSM*, p. 41), Susanna Moodie dares to question her membership among the invaders, among the planters, who "deny the ground they stand on" (*JSM*, p. 16). Unlike them, she is vulnerable, "broken / in upon" (*JSM*, p. 17). Helpless to impose her "human / architecture" (*JSM*, p. 22), she is instead "crept in / upon by green" (*JSM*, p. 26).

Denying himself Moodie's vulnerability, man controls all space and its geometries and incorporates woman's world into his domain. To draw near and meet the other in his monstrous body is fatal:

> Your face is silver
> and flat, scaled like a fish
>
> The death you bring me
> is curved . . .

(PP, p. 56)

Consummation is death:

> your mouth is nothingness
> where it touches me I vanish . . .

(PP, p. 53)

Speech, the third operation, loses its potential to name and create a word. Language instead is thick and heavy with violence. The words of woman's mouth are made to vanish, to become merely "a white comic-strip balloon / with a question mark; or a blank button" (*PU*, p. 45). She is nameless: "I can't tell you my name: / you don't believe I have one" (*PP*, p. 54), and trapped in his network of definitions: "I can feel you nailing STOP signs / all over my skin on the inside" (*PU*, p. 45). She cannot manifest herself in words; she is "a word / in a foreign language" (*JSM*, p. 11), a sound that cannot be heard in "this area where my damaged / knowing of the language means / prediction is forever impossible" (*JSM*, p. 15). She cannot discern the signals that delineate the trail.

In his complementary function in the circle game, man speaks his human order as the map of the universe. He repudiates the seeming randomness of the natural order by establishing himself as the centre. He memorizes names "to hold / these places / in their proper places" (*CG*, p. 39), wilfully blind to the flux and namelessness beneath and around him, as

> Things
> refused to name themselves; refused
> to let him name them.

(AC, p. 39)

He burdens words with his assertions of control, so that they become vampires, heavy instruments of empire. He is ignorant of the fragility and transcience of words, their "flight" (*CG*, p. 20).

On the other hand, Susanna Moodie is powerless, and hence retains her innocence regarding the creative power of speech. She knows that one must speak with the double voice of equivocal knowledge: one voice knows manners and hushed tones, the other a harsher truth. This double-speaking, however, tears her world:

> I began to forget myself
> in the middle
> of sentences. Events
> were split apart
>
> (*JSM*, p. 55)

Woman can construct a new word of truth only from within the anonymity of the smiling mask of femininity. It provides, in the blank distance between its skin and hers, a safe zone from within which to speak. In its empty interior she is innocent, free for new stories and a "fresh beginning" (*THP*, p. 13). Man's mouth, however, speaks only darkness, "pushing / aside the light" (*PU*, p. 47). Language is as helpless as those whose weakness makes its use necessary, the others having the fist by which to proclaim themselves. It will still be seized as the instrument of control, until the very tissues of the flesh are transcribed as documents of patriarchal consciousness, rendering images of "The billboard lady" and "the grey man" (*CG*, p. 29).

These constituent elements of "woman" and "man" will not hold true in steady focus. Features dissolve; faces change shape. The field of the circle game nevertheless has the face of woman and man. They are this field which they mutually constitute in the dimensions of eye, body, and word.

Man possesses by sight, but woman's sight is pierced, her eyes excised. Man colonizes and consumes the flesh of woman and world; woman permits herself to be used as crucible. Man asserts his words against the refusal of things to be named and withholds from woman the name that she requires. Man is the self-projection he relays through woman; he is the illusion he creates in his seizure of her gift of reflection. He exists for his assertion of the truth of his own order, requiring her to be mapped. Woman is man's construction of her; she is what is necessary for this definition. She exists for her mirroring representation of him, held by his imposition of face before her eyes. In the circle game of power politics, man is violence, woman is violated.

The transformation of the circle game begins with the first statement of encirclement:

> I want to break
> these bones, your prisoning rhythms
>
> . . .
>
> all the glass cases,
>
> erase all maps,
>
> . . .

> I want the circle
> broken.
>
> (*CG*, p. 44)

What must be broken are "the closed rules of your games" (*CG*, p. 43) of dominance and helplessness, the framing mirror, the "organized instant" fixed by the glass eye of the camera man (*CG*, p. 45), the celluloid postures, the woman of mud, the "True Romances." The world created by man and woman through the operations of eye, body, and word must be transformed.

Transformation of the players and their games occurs in three different movements. The first shift of the field occurs as a passive translation to the place of another vision beyond and beneath the circle game. Beyond the chessboard empire,

> the land unrolls without landmark
> a meshing of green on green, the inner
> membrane of the gaping moment
> opening around a sun that is
> a hole burnt in the sky.
>
> (*CG*, p. 17)

That universe is mapless and unbounded. It is a place not so much of escape as of recognition of terror, where intuitions of the fearful are given flesh, made sensible to ear and eye, given form in totemic translation into animal codes:

> only the cold jewelled symmetries
> of the voracious eater
> the voracious eaten
>
> the dream creatures that glow
> [. . .]
> . . . all
> gaping jaws and famine
>
> (*CG*, p. 22)

Such visions, such alternate incarnations, function as a descent through the conventional categories in which woman exists, through the depthless surface of the window in the middle of the floor on which she can see "cardboard figures / of myself" (*PU*, p. 21). They throw into suspension man's illusions of safety that trap speech and cast doubt upon illusions of solidity that keep man's body intact. Although the realm of this other zodiac can be entered and knowledge gained about "these wars" (*CG*, p. 23), it exists just barely tangent to this day, this city, this field of the circle game. Woman surfaces from its depths, breaks the membrane which encloses it, and returns to the circle game. In this realm, there is no transformation of the players and operations of the game.

A second movement of transformation can, however, attempt a permanent renewal of the world and its operations of construction. This movement begins with the shattering of illusions of safety and solidity. Knowing "I need wolf's eyes to see / the truth" (*JSM*, p. 13), refusing the futile preoccupation with "form, geometry, the human / architecture" (*JSM*, p. 22), Susanna Moodie permits her vulnerability to become a means of transformation. She risks the accompanying destruction of that unboundedness as she denounces man's illusion of solidity and allows herself to be "surrounded, stormed, broken / in upon" (*JSM*, p. 17). She opens her sight to "these trees, to this particular sun" (*JSM*, p. 17), rather than imposing her own order as seer upon the seen, even though this freedom of vision requires an excision of self:

> I take this picture of myself
> and with my sewing scissors
> cut out the face.
>
> [. . .]
>
> where my eyes were
> every-
> thing appears
>
> (*JSM*, p. 7)

She is consumed viscerally by what she sees, by the green and the animals.

This totemic metamorphosis to non-human flesh is not complete in the bush. Transformation of vision continues in her, breaking the architecture of the face, as is visible in the "Daguerrotype Taken in Old Age" (*JSM*, p. 48). Her human physiognomy of touch and sight is destroyed:

> Fiery green, my fingers
> curving and scaled, my
>
> opal
>   no
>   eyes glowing
>
> (*JSM*, p. 49)

Susanna Moodie has not only refused to participate in the human game of dominance but has taken her function in that game — availability, plasticity, and unboundedness — to the point where it breaks the game.

This action constitutes a flight of transcendence. In such transcendence there can be perfect communion between seer and seen, between visible surfaces and interior thought and feeling, between the speaker and the spoken. Water is no longer an instrument of duplicitous reflection but a medium of transformation of light. When we are "the water / itself" (*PU*, p. 37), the mechanism of seeing no longer intrudes.

To transcend the captivating hold of reflections and refractions, "to move beyond the mirror's edge," yields freedom for man "to pronounce / your own flesh" (*YAH*, p. 91). To transcend the postures and images of the sexual circle game yields "an undivided space" for woman and man where they can embrace in spontaneous warmth (*YAH*, p. 95). When words become no longer the "syntax of chained pebbles / but liquid" (*PU*, p. 69), man and woman can also "Take off the signatures" (*PP*, p. 50), the lies, alternate versions, and verbal reifications. Words will not speak in the lying double voice of the oppressed. They will pour forth from the power of brokenness in a leap toward a primal existence before language, toward the revelation of the body's plenitude before speech; at

> the melting point of granite
> when the bones know
> they are hollow & the word
> splits & doubles & speaks
> the truth & the body
> itself becomes a mouth.
>
> (*TS*, p. 64)

They will acquire the power to speak authentically and to accomplish what they say. In a pivotal utterance, woman freely speaks the proclamation that shatters the circle game:

> . . . the circle
> forming, breaking . . .
> [. . .]
>   transformed
>   for this moment /   always
> (because I say)
>
> the sea   the shore
>
> (*PU*, p. 79)

Although the circle game is transformed, although the operations of perception, expression and action are transformed into synaesthetic ecstasy ("light is a sound /

it roars / it fills us"), this transformation is accomplished only insofar as "we / are abolished" (*PU*, p. 76).

The third movement of transformation begins beyond the realm of the circle game, in the space of freedom and ecstasy gained by the second movement. Woman is the subject and agent of this movement of transformation. She moves beyond her function as mute and mirroring object, beyond her leap of transcendence, and assumes her historical identity as woman:

> As for the women, who did not
> want to be involved, they are involved.
>
> It's that blood on the snow
> which turns out to be not
> some bludgeoned or machine-gunned
> animal's, but your own
> that does it.
>
> (*THP*, p. 83)

The recognition of blood is crucial in this third movement of transformation, and crucial for a feminist reading of Atwood.

Identifying with this history, as woman, requires recognizing oneself as a being whose flesh is colonized, whose eyes are captured behind mirrors, whose words are helpless. After the plastic poses are shattered and knowledge is gained of alternate visions, after all instruments of touch, sight, and speech are renounced in favour of ecstatic revelation, escape from the circle game finally comes through bearing one's identity in grief. Only in this way can woman become the agent of history rather than its victim.

Woman discovers herself in the bloodline of women, "the procession / of old leathery mothers,/ . . . a long thread of red blood, not yet broken" (*THP*, p. 103). Matriarchal guides in this bloodline take several forms. The first guides can only display or proclaim their nothingness. The "necessary sibyl" remembers anguish and despair "safely bottled" for the woman who can only say "I don't care" (*CG*, p. 51). The "Ancestress: the burning witch" (*TS*, p. 64) is similarly mute, though not by her choice. And the woman from the water only stands and watches "through the eyes which were empty holes"(*PU*, p. 19).

Circe is a paradoxical image. She discloses the monstrousness of men but disowns it, preferring men in a different image, with "real faces and hands" (*YAH*, p. 47). She retains the mirroring function but reverses the relationship of power inherent in it, although she is unable to command man's transformation. She pronounces for him the "many things I want / you to have" (*YAH*, p. 54), but also has broken words torn from her in abrupt and incomplete confession. She is bound within his ruthless story which leaves her wordless: "when you leave will you give me back the words?" (*YAH*, p. 68) While she is Circe, agent of transformation, she is also the Mud Woman, object of manipulation.

Finally, the "black stone mother god" becomes the icon which enables woman to discover her own image:

> Worship what
> you like, what you want
> to be like . Old mother . . . .
>
> (*THP*, p. 90)

In identification with those bodies "with one more entrance than the world finds safe" (*THP*, p. 83), for whom "red is our colour by birth- / right, the colour of tense joy / & spilled pain that joins us / to each other"(*THP*, p. 103), woman breaks the circle game in which she was prisoner of man's enclosure.

Woman enters a new field of existence, constituted by new operations of eye, word, and body. She sees neither celluloid reflections nor ecstatic light, but painful facts which she must "see clearly and without flinching, / without turning away" (*TS*, p. 69). Her eyes are wrenched from their cool and glassy function as mirrors and are instead "taped open / two inches from the sun" (*TS*, p. 69). Freedom from the circle game requires seeing the truth: "Witness is what you must bear" (*TS*, p. 69).

This truth must also be spoken, and speech is freed from its helplessness to name the history of women. Stories will be told to make believable those things that happen "which cannot be believed and which are true" (*THP*, p. 49). Speech now asserts itself in strength: "A word after a word / after a word is power" (*TS*, p. 64), and will counsel ruthlessness and truth, "Iron talismans, and ugly, but / more loyal than mirrors"(*THP*, p. 84).

At the same time, flesh and its desires are restored to speech, and the "vowels plump / again like lips or soaked fingers" (*TS*, p. 26), the mouth says those vowels "again and again in wonder / and pain" (*TS*, p. 83). Language is no longer the imperialist assertion of order but the more vulnerable "message from the flayed tongue / to the flayed ear" (*THP*, p. 31), subsuming also the dream of transcendent, aqueous speech. The word becomes finite, precarious, enigmatic, based only upon the fragile being of the speaker, "your first naming, your first name, / your first word" (*TS*, p. 64). Poetry is made with the power of care and equally with the knowledge of limits:

> Against the disappearance
> of outlines, against
> the disappearance of sounds,
> against the blurring of the ears
> and eyes . . .

[. . .]

I make this charm
from nothing but paper; which is good
for exactly nothing.

(*THP*, p. 39)

Only because the transience and helplessness of the charm is recognized at the same time as it is made is the word free from imperialism.

As words become a living tissue "like the mouths / that hold and release / it" (*THP*, p. 67), flesh and its postures become finite and transparent. Life that is lived with "the smells / of cooking earth" (*THP*, p. 32) subsumes both the infinite monstrosity of masculine generativity and the ecstatic rhythm of the dance. What is celebrated is not Susanna Moodie's light-filled resurrection into the green vision, but everyday work, gestures of fingers, arms, muscles working with the earth and its elements. Everyday work, woman's work. In a final reversal of postures of dominance, gifts that the earth has given are received:

But the apples condense again
out of nothing on their stems
like the tree bleeding; something
has this compassion.

(*THP*, p. 92)

The connection is affirmed between what is given by the earth and what is constituted through human operation, in an image of mutuality that extends to woman and man. The perceptions, words, and gestures that constitute the world, and within it the field of sexual intersubjectivity, become the means not only of construction but of consecration:

Lift these ashes
into your mouth, your blood;
to know what you devour
is to consecrate it,
almost. All bread must be broken
so it can be shared. Together
we eat this earth.

(*THP*, p. 109)

As all consecrations are, this one too is founded in blood. Woman, who was colonized in the circle game, becomes the means of its transformation.

Notes

1. The "circle game" as central motif in Atwood has been noted before, as has its association with enclosures and garrisons: see, for example, Rosemary Sullivan, "Breaking the Circle," *Malahat Review* 41 (1977): 30–41, and Tom Marshall, "Atwood Under and Above Water," ibid., 89–94. For Sullivan and Marshall, the "circle game" functions in the construction of a Canadian myth and more generally in the construction of a self in the modern world.

2. For presentation of a phenomenological perspective, see Maurice Merleau-Ponty, *The Visible and the Invisible*, ed. Claude Lefort, trans. Alphonso Lingis (Evanston: Northwestern University Press, 1968), pp. 3–49 and 130–55; and *Signs*, trans. Richard C. McCleary (Evanston: Northwestern University Press, 1964), especially the "Introduction," pp. 14–22; "On the Phenomenology of Language," pp. 84–97; "Man and Adversity," pp. 224–43. Consider also the following: "The phenomenological world is not pure being, but the sense which is revealed where the paths of my various experiences intersect and engage each other like gears. It is thus inseparable from subjectivity and intersubjectivity, which find their unity when I either take up my past experiences in those of the present or other people's in my own" (*Phenomenology of Perception*, trans. Colin Smith [London: Routledge and Kegan Paul, 1965], p. xx).

3. Merleau-Ponty, *Signs*, p. 88.

4. Merleau-Ponty, *The Visible and the Invisible*, pp. 130-55. The openness of the self to other selves is a central problem in Merleau-Ponty's phenomenology. Although the visible and the tangible permeate both self and other and form the basis for communication between them, the doubling of the body as both touching and touched, seeing and seen, forms the basis for a fundamental fissure and segregation between self and other. Merleau-Ponty describes the meeting between seer and seen "as upon two mirrors facing one another where two indefinite series of images set in one another arise which belong really to neither of the two surfaces, since each is only the rejoinder of the other, and which therefore form a couple, a couple more real than either of them. Thus since each seer is caught up in what he sees, it is still himself he sees: there is a fundamental narcissism of all vision" (p. 139).

5. Cf. Lorraine Weir's discussion of the politics of perception in "Meridians of Perception: A Reading of *The Journals of Susanna Moodie*," in *The Art of Margaret Atwood*, ed. A. and C. Davidson, (Toronto: Anansi, 1980), pp. 69–79.

6. Paolo Freiere, *The Pedagogy of the Oppressed*, trans. Myra Bergman Ramos (New York: Herder and Herder, 1970), pp. 19–55. Consider especially the following: "One of the basic elements of the relationships between oppressor and oppressed is *prescription*. Every prescription represents the imposition of one man's choice upon another, transforming the consciousness of the man prescribed into one that conforms with the prescriber's consciousness. Thus, the behaviour of the oppressed is a prescribed behaviour, following as it does the guidelines of the oppressor" (p. 31).

7. John Wilson Foster, "The Poetry of Margaret Atwood," *Canadian Literature* 74 (1977): 5–20. Foster accuses Atwood of a "cultivation of barely controlled hysteria" which takes "specifically feminine forms" (p. 5) without anywhere documenting his charge. He would also charge her with "opportunism" in her involvement with the "minority psyche" except that he finds in her themes a coherence "deeper than minority membership" (p. 5); presumably one is an individual more truly than one is woman or Canadian. He does not note the irony of describing half the human species as a "minority" group. If Foster understood the voice in "Corpse Song" as the voice of woman killed by man, he would not wonder as he does about Atwood's ambivalence toward the female form. He would understand that its "phagic receptivity" (p. 13) is problematic in its vulnerability to masculine violence.

8. Sullivan, "Breaking The Circle," pp. 30–31.

9. Pierre Machéry, *A Theory of Literary Production*, trans. Geoffrey Wall (London: Routledge and Kegan Paul, 1978). By "condition of possibility," Machéry, a Marxist philosopher, means "not the empirical cause of a process, preceding it in a relationship of cause to effect; it is in fact the principle without which this process could not become an object of knowledge" (p. 10). The literary work is a "product" of a "real labour of production . . . *in determinate conditions*" (pp. 67–68), conditions which include the historical situation and individual existence of the writer as

well as the theoretical and ideological uses of language and the history of literary production (pp. 53, 71).
10. Cf. Lorraine Weir, " 'Fauna of Mirrors': The Poetry of Hébert and Atwood," *ARIEL* 10, (1979): 99–113, where the phenomenology of mirroring is discussed at length.
11. Merleau-Ponty, *Signs*, pp. 227–28, 231–32.
12. Ibid., p. 229: "The body is enigmatic: a part of the world, certainly, but offered in a bizarre way as its dwelling . . . [in] an absolute desire to draw near the other person and meet him in his body too, animated and animating, the natural face of the mind."

4

Atwood's Poetic Politics

Eli Mandel

Despite widespread agreement among readers and critics that Margaret Atwood is not only a major poet but very likely the best poet writing in Canada today, surprisingly few agree on the precise nature of her poetic achievement or the character of her work. There is little doubt that she focuses on social and psychological questions of particularly vivid contemporary concern and that she manages to provide these with both mythic and cultural resonance of a kind they have not usually attained so that her work takes on a peculiarly exemplary quality. As Rosemary Sullivan remarks, "Atwood clearly believes that the poet speaks simultaneously from a private and cultural or civic consciousness," writing as if, as was said of Whitman, "the function of the poet in the most radical and primitive sense of the word . . . is to give a nation a certain focal centre in the consciousness of its own character."[1] Yet, if it is commonly held that Atwood speaks out of a very real sense of the importance of contemporary social metaphors and social concern, still there is a widespread feeling too that she "explores certain fashionable minority psychologies"[2] and that some of her attractiveness derives from her exploitation of peculiarities at the edge of things rather than commonalities at the centre. Her voice has been described as "barely controlled hysteria,"[3] for example, and just as often as she is praised for her "extraordinary assurance of tone" and her "kind of sharp laconic discipline,"[4] we hear of "a wry stoic mask" that "covers a prolonged scream of pain."[5] True, the last refers to a narrator rather than to Atwood herself, who seldom if ever could be said to scream; nonetheless, it points to an oddity in the kind of response she evokes. There is no real accord concerning her tone or attitude, her point of view. She is described as either at the edge or the centre. She is, we have been told, a cultural nationalist and feminist, but equally a kind of cultural anthropologist exploiting the more esoteric concerns of some of our native peoples. To some, she appears as a quasi-Marxist, to others as an existential phenomenologist. Her interests are primitivist and equally modernist; she is intrigued or obsessed by agrophobia and also "dermophobia (or is it dermophilia)"; she shows "ambivalence toward . . . phagic receptivity" and some attraction to shamanic anthropology. "By now," says Robert Fulford, "it's difficult to separate Atwood the 'real' poet, novelist, publicist, from the various Atwoods of our imagination, the Atwoods we may have created to satisfy our cultural needs as these have arisen. Feminist, nationalist, literary witch, mythological poet, satirist, formulator of critical theories."[6]

Two sorts of questions arise out of these uncertainties. One, which to a degree involves content, has to do with Atwood's range of concerns with what has been called "minority psychologies" and the extent to which she is able to bring those into that kind of central focus Rosemary Sullivan writes of. From this, of course, a web of other questions spins out: is the centrality which we feel in a poet writing about the consciousness of national character finally what we think of as the genuinely major quality of a writer, or does it represent as peculiar a deflection from the poetic centre as, say, the elaboration of a minority psychology? Is there a distinction to be made between transformation and identity or should these also be in some profound way related, and, if so, does that relationship have to do not only with personal identity but with national identity? The second set of questions, to some extent following from the first, has to do with how the kinds of transformation that alter the peripheral or peculiar or minority concern can be understood. Are these poetic metamorphoses, and, if so, do they have more to do with what we commonly speak of as "technique" and "form" than "content"? Are the significant alterations in Atwood's perception of being and identity formal, and to that extent a question of technique, or rather the result of what has been called "a peculiar force of control," a consequence of "the essential coherence of Atwood's poetic themes"?[7]

If the first set of questions raises the issue of "mystification" and the linguistic and poetic means of handling that, the second comes closer to what in Atwood's work is more frequently than not called magic (with an attempt to give some precision to the use of that term), or otherwise, "shamanism." In the final analysis, the two lead to an area which is central to her work: the politics of poetry.

Throughout Atwood's seven books of poetry there are images of reflection: water, mirrors, glass, cameras, photographs, movies, and so on. This is not the only set of recurrences in her work: enclosed shapes and spaces, rooms, houses, doors, have been commented on, and of course there are others, poetic transformations (especially man-animal transformations), witch-woman figures, totemic men; but certainly among the most striking are her mirrors. *You Are Happy*, for example, offers an intriguing set of "Tricks with Mirrors." It is the mirror poems that suggest, more pointedly than usual in her work, questions about duplicity and reflexiveness and techniques of demystification — concerns quite different from apparently clear and accessible social comment. She writes:

Don't assume it is passive
or easy, this clarity

with which I give you yourself.
Consider what restraint it

takes: . . .

It is not a trick either,
It is a craft:

mirrors are crafty.

[. . .]

You don't like these metaphors
All right:

Perhaps I am not a mirror.
Perhaps I am a pool.

Think about pools.

(*YAH*, pp. 26-27)

The craft or craftiness of the mirror for Atwood is the degree to which it asserts by denial and so offers the possibility of transformation. The mirror demystifies itself. It is a craft, not a trick. The craft of poetry is the transformation of mirrors into pools. Reading the poem as if it were tricks and "metaphors" one is led, first, toward a series of false assumptions, mostly allegorical. Quite likely the speaker of the poem is meant to be taken as a lover; certainly she speaks to a Narcissus gazing at her as if she were a mirror; and to hear in the voice the artist's warning about craftiness may seem only a false clue (though it turns out to be genuine), and because the suggestion of allegory is so tempting in Atwood's work, it is difficult to resist. In any event, the poem, in this case through the mirror's voice, presents ambiguous possibilities that call to mind the contradictory qualities in Atwood's writing with which I began: clarity and accessibility, certainly, combined with an extraordinary deftness in manipulating contemporary modes of speech and image, a compelling toughmindedness, a ruthless unsentimentality, somehow liberating rather than cynically enclosing ("Don't you get tired of saying Onward?" Circe asks Ulysses, and she comments, "Men with the heads of eagles / no longer interest me"); but, apparently pointing to social concerns, these modes and attitudes may very well conceal quite different attitudes. Like mirrors, oracles tend to speak gnomically: "Consider what restraint it / takes." Perhaps the oracular deserves rather more extended commentary than it has received in Atwood's writing. I am thinking of the Gothic elements of her poetry, her consistent and obsessive use of reduplicating images, and her totemic or transforming images of journey and spirit; those devices I would group under the heading: techniques of demystification.[8]

Her first seven volumes of poetry reveal a quite unusual consistency of approach and unity of preoccupation, an essential thematic coherence pointed up particularly by the *Selected Poems*. "Underlying connections deeper than minority membership" as individual, woman, and Canadian, John Wilson Foster argues, "flesh out in multiple guise the root formula of her poetry."[9] It is his special achievement to draw attention to her poetics of space, "the self's inhabitation of space and form and the metamorphoses entailed therein" and all the thematically important derivations from this: "invasion, displacement, evolution and reversion" as well as the perhaps more important notions "survival, ingestion . . . and surfacing." The primary movement of these books is through a series of journeys, either inward or downward, accompanied by transformations that culminate in "Songs of the Transformed" and the "Circe/Mud Poems." Surprisingly, the "Two-Headed Poems" (from the collection of that title), which one might expect to make a good deal of the monstrousness of twins joined at the head, tends to treat the deformity as mere political allegory rather than the usual "myths and images of the secret self," as Fiedler would speak of it. Since aside from a somewhat witty colloquialism and lexis of pop-cult there are relatively few surprises in diction or in syntax in *Two-Headed Poems*, the unusual strength of this nexus of imagery must lie elsewhere, in a series of reversals about outside and inside, the fantastic and the real, the ghost-like and the substantial, the mirror or reduplicating poetics I referred to earlier.

Atwood's comment, in a conversation with Graeme Gibson, that *Surfacing* "is a ghost story" provides the point of departure for more than one commentary on her work. Less often noticed is the special form of ghost story Atwood employs, the story in *The Journals of Susanna Moodie*, for example. No doubt, Moodie, like other haunted and haunting Atwood figures, suffers a kind of wilderness trauma so that she is one with such figures as those in "After the Flood, We," "Progressive Insanities of a Pioneer," "Journey to the Interior," and even "The Reincarnation of Captain Cook." Mrs. Moodie appeared to Atwood, she says, in a dream, later manifesting herself "as a mad-looking and very elderly lady"; the poems take her "through an estranged old age, into death and beyond" (*JSM*, p. 63). That makes her a ghost in the last poem, "A Bus Along St. Clair: December," where she tells us:

> I am the old woman
> sitting across from you on the bus,
> her shoulders drawn up like a shawl;
> out of her eyes come secret
> hatpins, destroying
> the walls, the ceiling

(*JSM*, p. 61)

Her earthly life, portrayed in the earlier poems, involves a pattern not unlike the heroine's journey into the backwoods in *Surfacing*: a landing on a seashore apparently occupied by dancing sandflies, a pathway into a forest, confrontation with a wolfman and other animals, men in masks, deaths of children, including a drowning, sinister plants. Gothic tale is a better name than ghost story for this form, in which the chief element is a threat to a maiden, a young girl, a woman. In a well-known passage Leslie Fiedler comments on the chief elements of the form, its motifs: the Maiden in flight, the haunted countryside, the haunted castle or abbey, dark passages, cavernous apartments.[10]

Substitute forest for castle and think of the ghosts of Mrs. Radcliffe's *The Italian* and the ghost story or Gothic form of the typical Atwood novel and poem begins to take shape. Obviously, there are displacements: the threat of unstructured or unmapped space is more sinister and alarming than ruins; the "malignant face" is of the forest, not the dark man who represents power; there are psychic hazards in space of this kind subtly examined in Foster's account of spatial metaphors, the tension of inner and outer in Atwood's poems, the peculiar mind-body dislocations (physically here, psychically there).[11] To be sure, the pattern is richly suggestive of a variety of dark threats, either psychological or hidden in the social structure. It is interesting to notice that Atwood's Moodie is a mythic figure. While the historical Moodie became a successful lady of letters in a decent Ontario town, the pioneer of Atwood's poems lives a more perilous life in a landscape offering possibilities of allegory and the richly creative pattern of psychic journey.

A further elaboration of Gothic possibilities is suggested by Ellen Moers' comments in the chapter of her *Literary Women* called "The Female Gothic." Gothic, says Moers, is writing that "has to do with fear," writing in which "fantasy predominates over reality, the strange over the commonplace, and the supernatural over the natural, with one definite auctorial intent: to scare. Not, that is, to reach down into the depths of the soul and purge it with pity and terror (as say tragedy does) but to get to the body itself, its glands, muscles, epidermis, and circulatory system, quickly arousing and quickly allaying the physiological reactions to fear."[12] Moers' emphasis on physiological effect seems appropriate. It points to the kind of imagination found, say, in Michael Ondaatje's work as well as in Atwood's that might appropriately be called a physiological imagination.[13] It lends credence too to Foster's otherwise odd argument that "It is the skin, that membraneous edge between inside and outside, by which Atwood is especially fascinated, though it sometimes takes the form of outlines, margins or surfaces."[14] The sexual aspect of this Foster touches on, though he takes no note of its resemblance to Cohen's polymorphous perversity or the ancient tradition that angels copulate by commingling throughout nor does he develop further the question of borders, a matter of some importance in understanding techniques of demystification.

Fear. But fear of what? Some say sexuality, especially taboo aspects of sexuality, incest for example: the Gothic threat to a young woman carries implications of sado-masochistic fantasy, the victim/victor pattern of *Survival* (it is sometimes forgotten that, as Atwood herself points out, the phrase derives from the highly suggestive title of Michael Charters' novel).[15] Ellen Moers suggests that in Mary Shelley's *Frankenstein*, the real taboo is birth itself, death and birth hideously mixed in the creation of a monster out of pieces of the human body. (The image involves, as well, the hideousness of duplication and reduplication, a quality Borges is careful to point out in his "Tlön, Uqbar, Orbis Tertius" and elaborated in a study of the Freudian significance of Borges' mirrors in Emir Roderiquez Monegal's biography, *Jorge Luis Borges*.) In Atwood's "Speeches for Dr. Frankenstein," her Dr. Frankenstein addresses his creation in unmistakable language about a botched creation, a birth/death confusion.

> I was insane with skill:
> I made you perfect.
>
> I should have chosen instead
> to curl you small as a seed,
>
> trusted beginnings. Now I wince
> before this plateful of results:
>
> core and rind, the flesh between
> already turning rotten.
>
> I stand in the presence
> of the destroyed god:
>
> a rubble of tendons,
> knuckles and raw sinews.
>
> Knowing that the work is mine
> how can I love you?
>
> (*AC*, p. 44)

If, as he says to his monster, Dr. Frankenstein might have trusted in beginnings, in seed, Atwood as narrator, it seems, distrusts virtually all births. There are "The Deaths of Other Children" in the *Journals*, "The Foundling" contemplating his scars, and of course all the drownings like inverted births, from the opening poem of her second book, "This is a Photograph of Me" through "Death of a Young Son by Drowning" to "Younger Sister, Going Swimming" which, like the photograph of the first poem, re-enacts a primal surfacing scene. Most notably there are the dolls of *Two-Headed Poems*, those from the land of the unborn, the "lost children, / those who have died or thickened / to full growth and gone away" (p. 19). As in the pattern of mixed birth/death in *Surfacing*, we begin to see the ghosts: the baby not born, the baby aborted, the baby about to be born as a furred monster, the drowned brother who did not drown, the baby peering out of the mother's stomach, the embryo-like frogs, the frog-like embryos, the man-frog father in the waters, hanging from the camera with which he might have photographed the gods.

Who are the ghosts of Atwood's poetry then? The answer goes a long way toward explaining the poetic process of demystification and especially toward locating the means by which Atwood's consistent attention to articulating a minority position focuses her work on complex symbols of wider application than they first appear to possess, particularly in social and cultural history. In *Survival*, which reads like a gloss on *Surfacing* (though Atwood hints the chronology goes the other way around), Atwood tells us that the ghost or death goddess of *The Double Hook* represents fear, but not fear of death, fear of life. And babies? Following a rather horrendous list of miscarriages, cancers, tumours, stillbirths and worse, which she finds in Canadian novels, she remarks laconically, "The Great Canadian Baby is sometimes alarmingly close to the Great Canadian Coffin" (p. 208). Fear of life. It is possible to read R. D. Laing's social phenomenology in *The Politics of Experience* as a commentary or gloss on Atwood's use of the invisible world in her poetry, particularly because of the Laingian handling of supposed distinctions between "inner" and "outer" and his account of the devastation or mystification of experience, estrangement, alienation from oneself, the shrivelling up of the reality in which one is lodged. Simply, Laing suggests the reality of inner or invisible experience, a suggestion that at once defines ghosts as experience:

> Experience is invisible to the other. But experience is not "subjective" rather than "objective," not "inner" rather than "outer," not process rather than praxis, not input rather than output, not psychic rather than somatic, . . . We seem to live in two worlds, and many people are aware only of the "outer" rump. As long as we remember that the "inner" world is not some space "inside" the body or mind, this way of talking can serve our purpose. . . . The "inner," then, is our personal idiom of experiencing our bodies, other people, the animate and inanimate world: imagination, dream, phantasy, and beyond that to ever further reaches of experience.[16]

The devastation of experience consists primarily of the ways in which by even a glance, gesture, or remark, we shrivel up reality. Aspects of it no longer exist, having become inner, mystified, de-realized. The genuine courage of Atwood's poetry is her reversal of this process of devastation, the reconstruction of a devastated world. This is not without terror. For one thing, it requires facing up to the ghosts: ghosts, sexual fears we say, repressed contents of the imagination, social rigidity. Ghosts, as the narrator says of her parents after her experience in the woods in *Surfacing*: "they dwindle, grow, become what they were, human. Something I never gave them credit for" (*Sfg.*, p. 220). Ghosts: only the human body, repressed, denied; only life denied. So all proceeds from the ghosts: a de-realized world: victimization, sexism, deformed sexuality, sado-masochism, tearing away at nature's body, at our own bodies. From the position of what Foster calls the "minority psyche," then, the "cultivation of barely controlled hysteria" or "the psychic individual at sea in a materialist society," a series of themes of major cultural concern develops through the language of the ghost story, Gothic romance. The invisible made visible as in "This is a photograph of Me," in *The Circle Game*. The power, of course, is in the utter literalness of language. There are, so to speak, no lies. At one level, this is a trick, a kind of insane phenomenology, a play with duplication (photographs, say); at another, it is a form of magic (one psychological term for which is synchronicity), of the occult, or shamanism:

> (The photograph was taken
> the day after I drowned.
>
> I am in the lake, in the center
> of the picture, just under the surface.
>
> It is difficult to say where
> precisely, or to say
> how large or small I am:
> the effect of water
> on light is a distortion
>
> but if you look long enough,
> eventually
> you will be able to see me.)

(*CG*, p. 11)

Scarcely a poem of Atwood's does not in some way allude to magic or sorcery. A random list produces the drowned-living ("This is a photograph of Me"), metamorphoses ("Eventual Proteus," not to mention "Circe/Mud Poems" and "Songs of the Transformed"), rites of exclusion ("The Circle Game"), portents and secret languages ("Migration: C.P.R."), totems ("Some Objects of Wood and Stone"), magical animals, either of the talking or ceremonial sort ("The Animals in That Country"), monsters ("Frankenstein," "The Wereman"), vampirism ("Disembarking at Quebec"), journeys underground ("Dream 1: The Bush Garden"), voodoo dolls and masks ("Midwinter, Presolstice," "Five Poems for Dolls"), prophecy ("Foretelling the Future"), amulets ("Digging"). The list can go on: it produces witch women like Circe, initiation rites, descents to the underworld, consecrated spaces, kratophanies, hierophanies, magical heat and magical fire, and sacred phrases. The geography of an Atwood poem is now well-known and recognizable: south is a place of sapped power, a wreckage of "the future," this rubble ("Two Headed Poems"); north, the interior, the wilderness, a threat, source of power. As an aside, it is worth noting that Atwood's magical wilderness has its predecessor not only in her own interest in ancestral power and its spirit world, but in the Group of Seven's interest in theosophy with its account of Canada as a cosmological centre; hence Lawren Harris' equation of north with spirit and the journey ever northward.[17] A parallel appears in Mary Shelley's *Frankenstein* with the monster's death in the Arctic. But though the magical concerns are equally well known, their precise function and pattern remains to be worked out. Magic, in fact, remains problematical in Atwood's work, for all its presence.

Normally, critics satisfy themselves with nominal gestures toward the occult as simply "atmosphere" or "mood," at best, probably metaphors for the really serious concerns of Atwood's work which are usually taken to be psychological and sociological. Those who have taken her totemic and metaphoric images seriously have sought their sources in cultural anthropology, noting rightly how much of the symbolism derives from North American tribal cults. Reviewing Atwood's *Selected Poems*, Woodcock remarks on "the consistency of her preoccupations and the unity of her work" and adds significantly, "I suppose the adjective that might throw most light on that consistency is 'shamanic.' "

> The ambiguous relationships between man and the animal world and the curious spiritual emanations of such relationships; the awarness of the mythical universality of transformation, which can move in any direction, so that men behave like animals as popular metaphors suggest, but animals in their turn display qualities we had thought of as a human monopoly; that war is love: such factors dominate a verse sequence like the "Circe/Mud Poems," but they also dominate Atwood's fiction, in the shamanic anthropophagy of *The Edible Woman* and in the equally shamanic regression-and-rebirth theme *of Surfacing*, while they are present in a work outside fiction and poetry like *Survival*.[18]

Extraordinarily suggestive of the major patterns and effects of Atwood's poetry as this is, Woodcock leaves unresolved the question of purpose. Is the highly developed art of metamorphosis here simply formal and technical (something often suggested by those of her readers who find her always "skilful" but not necessarily convincing, an artist of design rather than of passion and its accompaniment, "vision") or does it in some way connect with, develop, and comment on "content," the substance of her work?

It is perhaps not by the way that Rosemary Sullivan too notices the shamanic account in *Surfacing* of the critical state of entrancement the narrator undergoes in the wilderness, and comments on its correspondence "by coincidence or intent" with Mircea Eliade's account of shamanic initiation outlined in his study *Shamanism: Archaic Techniques of Ecstasy.*[19] The moment of ecstasy, it appears, is very close to what Eliade calls "separation," the moment that begins the shaman's "new, true life," a moment as Sullivan rightly notes that is "a process of induction into the sacred," "a spiritual crisis . . . not lacking in tragic greatness and in beauty."[20] But there is a puzzle here; one of some import to the significance of Atwood's work. The true shamanic moment occurs when, having undergone the crisis of separation, through hereditary transmission or "election" or "call," the shaman has singularity conferred on him. He is a receptacle for the manifestation of the sacred. But as Rosemary Sullivan notes, this is not the consequence of the narrator's experience in *Surfacing*:

> The question is, can these insights be integrated with normal consciousness. The answer is no. There is no bridge from this experience into the narrative present, and in the penultimate chapter, the narrator abandons her "questionable" gods . . . The narrator has come a long way toward healing herself. She has come to terms with her past and her posture of defencelessness: "This above all, to refuse to be a victim." She seems to have recognized that she cannot abdicate from history, or from society. But she has not broken the circle because she has not achieved spiritual regeneration.[21]

Whatever her experience, it cannot have been shamanic. Moral regeneration, as Sullivan correctly notes, is not spiritual (or sacred) regeneration, which would involve living her life sacramentally, as a series of rituals, and it might involve more: magical flights, fire mastery, dismemberment, ecstatic journeys; in other words, entry into the shamanic world.

What is to be made, then, of the "return to normality," a return which does not fully characterize the poetry written after *Surfacing* in which magical implications continue to present themselves. On the one hand, it is entirely possible that Woodcock and Sullivan are wrong to speak of "shamanism," convincing though the general thesis may be. On the other, Atwood may be offering her own alternatives to the apparently supernatural implications of magical incantations. A third possibility presents itself, a literary rather than anthropological or "spiritual" explanation.

The approach to Atwood through Laing's social phenomenology does offer an adequate account of how literary devices of duplication and Gothic romance can be used to reveal those invisible aspects of contemporary culture which have been de-realized or mystified. The kind of analysis applied here has particular meaning for *Power Politics*, on the one hand, and *The Journals of Susanna Moodie*, on the other. It has long seemed to me that "They Eat Out" in its play with role-playing is both the wittiest and most revealing of the *Power Politics* sequence; super-man vs. magic woman testing their mythic powers in an atmosphere of fried rice and pop culture. As for the *Journals*, the handling of history as myth and of ghost stories as the structural principle of the Canadian character strikes me as nothing less than superb. The audacity of choosing a mad old lady as the symbol of a country and its pioneer schizophrenia is perhaps no more surprising than that so many have read it as valid self-definition.

Magic substitutes chance for cause, synchronicity for causality. It employs randomness that plays havoc with notions of identity and opens the possibility of occult possession. And the invisible world seems to have special attractions for Atwood, just as totems and animals do. It is possible that what comes into existence where there appeared to be nothing is what should have been seen all along and what George Woodcock is right to speak of as the curious spiritual emanations of the ambiguous relationships between men and animals.

Atwood's use of the shamanic mode of demystification remains a possibility, at least in the metaphoric sense that she is willing to allow her poet-persona to present herself as sorcerer, healer, psychic traveller, if not astral being. However, the rather simpler possibility remains too that Atwood is willing to let the magical implications work as technical (or formal) devices, as the structural demands of poetry; her reading of Canadian "monsters" in her article in *The Canadian Imagination* suggests as much.[22] But, as John Cage notes in his "History of Experimental Music in the United States," "Sri Ramakrishna was once asked, 'Why, if God is good, is there evil in the world?' He said, 'In order to thicken the plot.' "[23] Similarly in Atwood, it may be that magic functions as a way of thickening the plot, as a demystifying device in itself. Perhaps from the point of view of one's estimate of Atwood's achievement, this is the preferable explanation of her techniques of demystification, her poetic politics.

Does Atwood use magic as a means of political comment? The suggestion is no longer as outrageous as it once seemed, given a prime minister who used a medium and loved ruins and given Lawren Harris' theosophical reading of Canada North, or for that matter given Robertson Davies' Jungian account of Canadian psychology or Gwendolyn MacEwen's esoteric reading of the lore and language of the wilderness. Can *Survival* be read in the light of shamanism, as Woodcock suggests, and, if so, is it poetry or that failure of nerve we call allegory?[24] Certainly, to look at her title sequence from *Two Headed Poems* is to fear such a failure. But this book offers two other poems that raise very different kinds of questions and suggest that any attempts at final answers about her work must be held in abeyance. Both poems, like so much of Atwood's work, are controlled, urgent, contemporary. One is "Footnote To The Amnesty Report on Torture," the other "Five Poems for Grandmothers." What is notable about these is that in both she uses her mastery to new and more mature effects. The "Amnesty" poem raises the most difficult political question that can be raised today: who is the torturer? No answer is proposed. The perspective is unusual, not original but striking. As I read her version of the dilemma, she says nothing that has not been said before. But she faces the dreadful question. Without melodrama. That alone is courage. Nothing fancy. The smell and taste and texture, the colour of it all. No one in this country is close yet to the South American writers, perhaps for obvious reasons.

The "grandmothers" (or is it just the one after all, the one standing for all of them) is a more remarkable poem. For here — and for virtually the first time — Atwood does what she has not done elsewhere. As before, as always, she starts with magic:

> It was once filled with whispers;
> it was once a horn
> you could blow like a shaman
> conjuring the year,
> and your children would come running.
>
> [. . .]
>
> The shell is now a cave
> which opens for you alone.
> It is still filled with whispers
> which escape into the room,
> even though you turn it mouth down.

(THP, p. 33)

But if she meant to turn the old woman into a magic creature, she obviously changed her mind. Movingly, profoundly, she gives it up. She writes a human poem. It is a woman's poem. It is deeply moving. The magic is gone:

> I make this charm
> from nothing but paper; which is good
> for exactly nothing.

(THP, p. 39)

Notes

1. Rosemary Sullivan, "Breaking the Circle," in "Margaret Atwood: A Symposium," *Malahat Review* 41 (1977): 30-31.
2. John Wilson Foster, "The Poetry of Margaret Atwood," *Canadian Literature* 74 (1977): 5.
3. Ibid., p. 5.
4. George Woodcock, "Playing with Freezing Fire," *Canadian Literature* 70 (1976): 85. See also Pat Sillers' "Power Impinging: Hearing Atwood's Vision," *Studies in Canadian Literature* 4 (1979): 59.
5. Rowland Smith, "Margaret Atwood: The Stoic Comedian," *Malahat Review* 41 (1977): 144.
6. Robert Fulford, "The Images of Atwood," *Malahat Review* 41 (1977): 95. Others referred to here are Woodcock and John Wilson Foster on the question of anthropophagy and dermophobia respectively; Rick Salutin, "A Note on the Marxism of Atwood's *Survival*," *Malahat Review* 41 (1977): 57-61; Gloria Onley, "Power Politics in Bluebeard's Castle," in *Poets and Critics*, ed. George Woodcock (Toronto: Oxford University Press, 1974), pp. 202–3, the most significant study of Atwood from the point of view of cultural anthropology.
7. Foster, "Poetry of Margaret Atwood," p. 5.
8. Demystification, discussed at length below, refers to the process — not unlike the Brechtian notion of alienation — of assertion by denial. See R. D. Laing's discussion in *The Politics of Experience* (New York: Ballantine Books Edition, 1968).
9. Foster, "Poetry of Margaret Atwood," p. 5.
10. *Love and Death in the American Novel* (New York: Meridian Books, 1962), pp. 111–12.
11. Foster, "Poetry of Margaret Atwood," p. 9.
12. *Literary Women* (New York: Doubleday, 1976), p. 90.
13. Like Atwood, Ondaatje, especially in *The Collected Works of Billy the Kid* and *Coming through Slaughter*, and Kroetsch in *The Studhorse Man* and *Badlands* tend to bring together images of sexuality, dismemberment, and poetics, poetic and sexual obsessions leading to anatomies.
14. Foster, "Poetry of Margaret Atwood," p. 12. The point bears development. It may be that Dennis Lee's *Savage Fields* skirts the same issue though with an odd shyness considering some of Lee's language in his essay on cosmology. Ann Mandel, who is writing on the subject in Canadian shorter fiction, draws my attention to Christopher Ricks' discussion of the sexuality of blushing in *Keats and the Literature of Embarrassment*.
15. Atwood cites Charters' novel *Victor/Victim* in the "Tributes" for *Survival*.
16. Laing, *Politics of Experience*, pp. 20–21.
17. The Group of Seven's theosophical interest is a point worth further discussion. I touch on it in my article, "The Inward, Northward Journey of Lawren Harris," *Arts Canada* (October-November, 1978): 17–24, in which I acknowledge the importance of Ramsay Cook's essay, "Landscape Painting and National Sentiment in Canada," in *The Maple Leaf Forever*, second edition (Toronto: Macmillan, 1977), and Ann Davis' Ph.D. thesis, "An Apprehended Vision: The Philosophy of the Group of Seven" (York University, 1973).
18. Woodcock, "Playing with Freezing Fire," p. 85.
19. Sullivan, "Breaking the Circle," p. 37. One regrets that the article by Germaine Warkentin, referred to in Sullivan's footnote, has not to my knowledge appeared in print. As Woodcock's allusions make clear, there is little doubt about the relevance of Eliade to a study of Atwood's metaphors, and her language, but the question of sources remains unresolved.
20. *Shamanism: Archaic Techniques of Ecstasy*, trans. William Trask (Princeton University Press, 1964), p. 13. Sullivan's account of shamanic initiation cites p. 64 of *Shamanism*. Oddly, she does not go on to p. 67 and the significant opening sentence of the next chapter on "Obtaining Shamanic Powers": "We have seen that one of the commonest forms of the future shaman's election is his

encountering a divine or semidivine being, who appears to him through a dream, a sickness, or some other circumstance, tells him he has been 'chosen,' and incites him thence forth to follow a new rule of life."

21. Sullivan, "Breaking the Circle," p. 39.
22. "Canadian Monsters: Some Aspects of the Supernatural in Canadian Fiction," in *The Canadian Imagination*, ed. David Staines (Cambridge, MA: Harvard University Press, 1977), pp. 97–122.
23. John Cage, "History of Experimental Music in the United States," *Silence* (London: Calder and Boyer, 1939), pp. 67–68.
24. Parts of this article appeared in my earlier "Atwood Gothic," in *Malahat Review* 41 (1977): 165-74, reprinted in *Another Time* (Toronto: Press Porcépic, 1977). My suggestion there that *Survival* might be read as a novel seemed to some critics either frivolous or amusing, though Atwood takes a rather different view: "Eli Mandel, of course, feels that all works of criticism are novels and in a way he's right. They *are* imaginative constructs." "Interview with Margaret Atwood," by Linda Sandler, *Malahat Reivew* 41 (1977): 22. So much for interviews and authorial comment.

Surface Structures:
The Syntactic Profile of *Surfacing*

Robert Cluett

As anyone knows who has been to one of her readings, the peculiar lingering flavour of Margaret Atwood's poetry read aloud derives only partly from the text and its brutally skewed ikons. What truly stays with one is the remarkable bleached voice from which all devices of oral colouring have been ruthlessly laundered: the reading is given with no variation in either pitch or volume and with as little provision of stress as the English language will allow; the ikons hang starkly in the air, suspended almost as though self-willed, with no specifically human intervention.

It is easy to suspect, at a second reading, that she has done in *Surfacing* a very similar thing with the non-phonological resources of the language, notably the syntactic resources, the retrenchment of which gives the book a syntactic profile that seems unique not only in the Atwood canon but in all twentieth century fiction. In no other author than Atwood and in no other book than *Surfacing* has the range of these resources been so drastically inhibited. It will be interesting to speculate on why such an *intended* fact (for so it appears) might manifest itself in a particular novel written in the artist's mid-career. But first to the real task of this kind of criticism: a description of the style and of the method used to adduce it.

The basis of the article that follows is five computerized syntactic profiles from the York Computer Inventory of Prose Style. The profiles each consist of a random sample of 3500 words of narrative and descriptive fiction text (no dialogue); the text is parsed and translated into a 98-slot word class grammar for computer processing; it is then analysed in a variety of ways by several computer programs.[1] The texts chosen for the present analysis are as follows:

9611 Morley Callaghan	*A Native Argosy* and *Strange Fugitive*
9615 Robertson Davies	*Fifth Business*
9618 Margaret Laurence	*The Stone Angel*
9613 Leonard Cohen	*The Favorite Game*
9662 Margaret Atwood	*Surfacing*

It is not hard to find the rationale for choosing the particular control writers: three of them are eminent Canadian contemporaries whose first language is English; the other is not quite a contemporary, but has been alleged, from time to time, to have been a major figure among the linguistic-retrenchers working in Paris in the 1920's in the penumbra of Gertrude Stein.

The comparisons among these five were revealing, showing the Atwood text to be truly distinctive in a wide variety of ways. An extension of the comparison to include the historical information on file with the Inventory and already published suggests that the text is unique to a degree even greater than first appears. The properties of the syntax of the York sample — its short clauses, its utter eschewing of modifying words, its pronominality, its clause-end additions (participials and appositives), its nearly total avoidance of subject-minus zeugmatic additioning[2] — add up to a style distinguished not merely by the magnitude of its deviations from the norm but also by their sheer number. In examining those deviations, I will proceed from the sentence down. In other words, I shall begin by considering the sentence (how its clauses are arrayed), and then move to clause structure, phrase structure, and word-class distributions.

CLAUSAL ARRAYS

Figure 1 shows for *Surfacing* and the four controls the disposition of full and half stops (that is, of periods and of internal full stops like colons, semi-colons, and commas used in standard semi-colon position). Within a relatively long period (nearly as long as those of the deliberately archaic Davies'[3] archaic Dunstan Ramsay), Atwood gives us an extraordinary number of internal full stops, the two kinds of stop — period and internal — coming at an interval of roughly every 12 words, the shortest such interval of any of our five samples. Similarly stunted are the average interval per finite clause[4] and the average interval per clause of any kind (figure 2). Though in the latter category Callaghan approaches her and in the former category Laurence's number is lower, the amount of subject-minus clause additioning in both the other writers suggests that Atwood in fact is generating the shortest clauses of the five writers.

Consideration of figure 3 (subject-minus co-ordinated clauses) is illuminating: the *normal* tendency in a novel would seem to be to add every sixth or eighth clause in the subject-minus way. With Callaghan, the process is frequent:

> She was scared of him and would have turned away but a man got out of a car at the curb and smiled at her. (9611, *Strange Fugitive*, p. 136)

FIGURE 1: FULL- and HALF STOPS

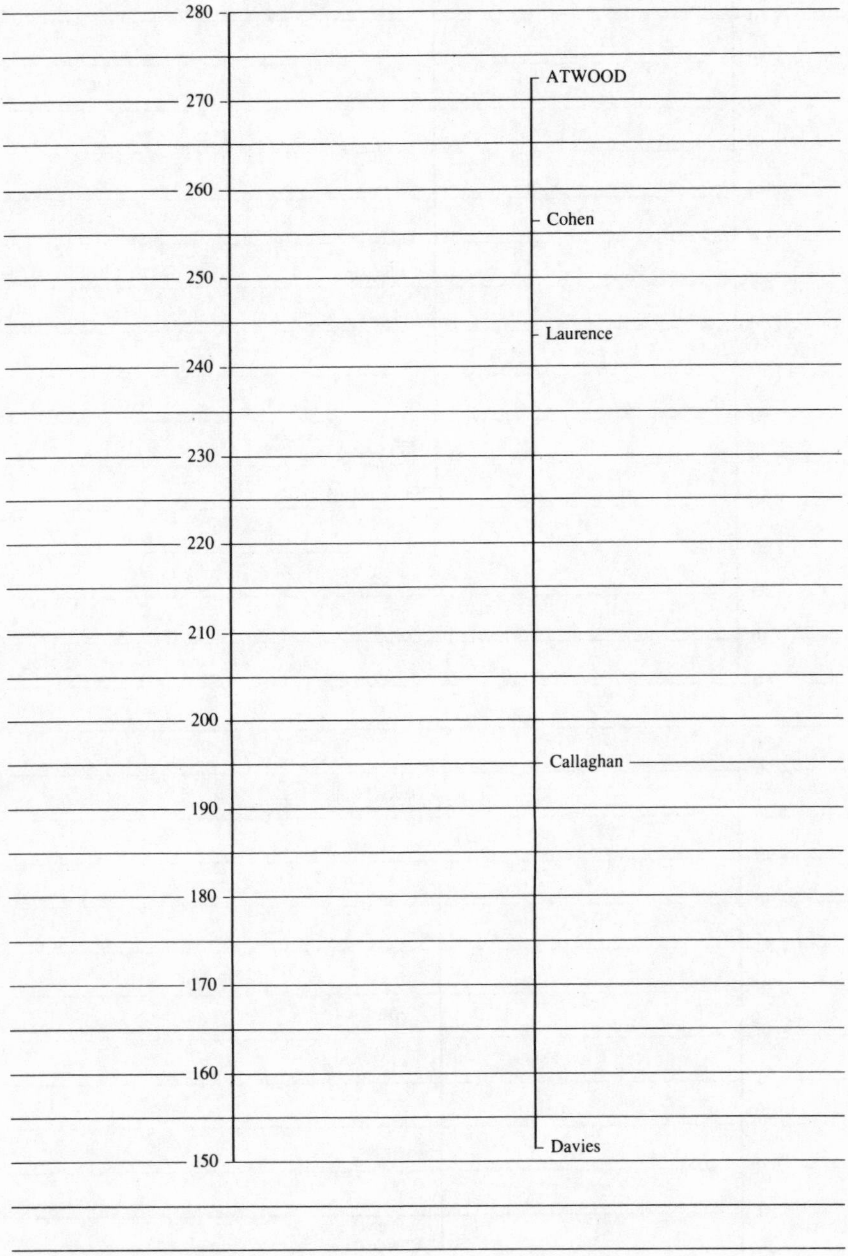

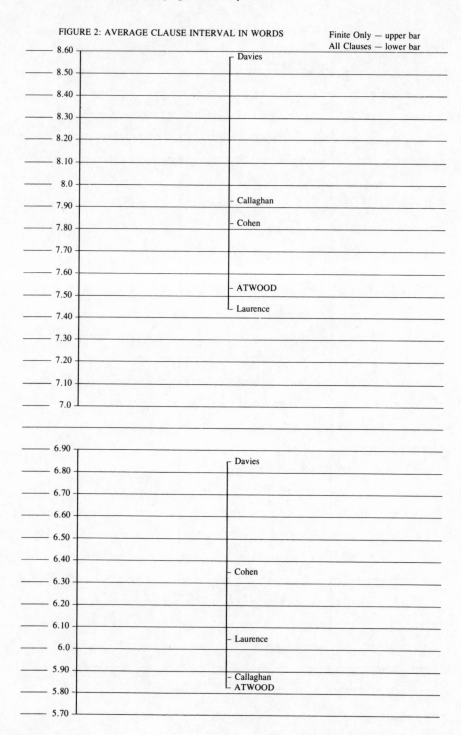

FIGURE 2: AVERAGE CLAUSE INTERVAL IN WORDS   Finite Only — upper bar
                                                    All Clauses — lower bar

FIGURE 3: SUBJECT-MINUS COORDINATED CLAUSES

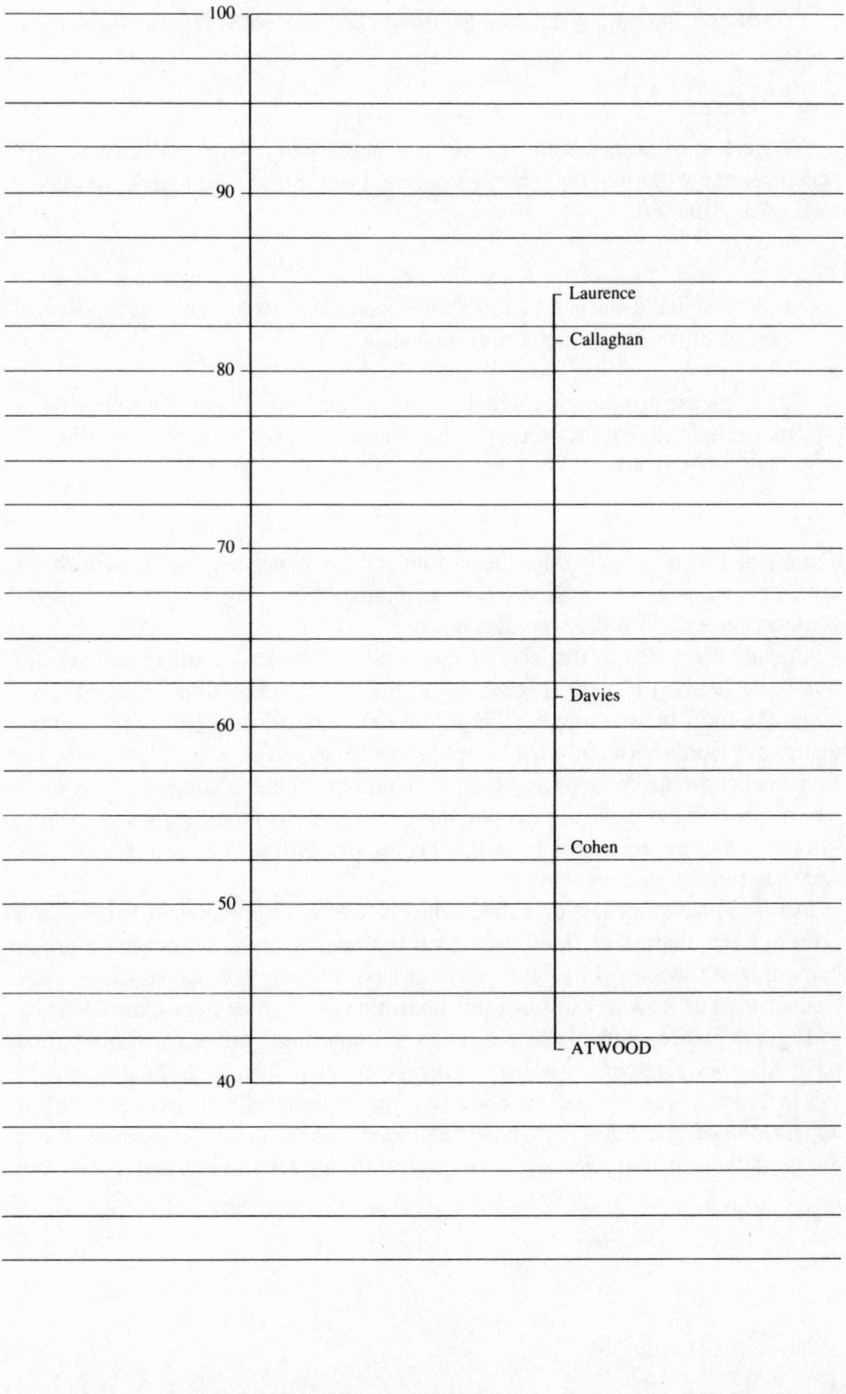

Similarly, with Laurence:

> He turned and put his hand on the doorknob . . . (9618, *The Stone Angel*, p. 130)

Notice that in both the above cases we have cited a four- and a two-clause sentence, one with two, the other with one subject-minus additioning. Atwood's method is different:

> I give David the machete, I don't know what shape the trail will be in, we may have to brush it out: Joe carries the hatchet.

> It's overcast, lowhanging cloud; there's a slight wind from the southeast, it may rain later or it may miss us, the weather here comes in pockets, like oil. (9662, *Sfg*, p. 46)

The method here is totally opposite — four and five clause sentences, each clause with its own subject, with no subject-minus additioning and only a single conjunction, the *or* in the second sentence.

Equally distinctive is the technique of arranging both subordinate clauses and non-finite (verbal) clauses. Figure 4 (location of first subordinate clause) illustrates the ratio between average point of first subordinate clause and average distance in words between stops.[5] The closer such a ratio came to 1.0, the stronger the evidence would be for a right-branched, terminally elaborating use of subordinate clauses. In the *Surfacing* sample, that ratio is .93, by far the highest of the five samples under scrutiny. In short, *Surfacing* uses subordinate clause in a disproportionately right-branching way.

An examination of left-branched sentence openings is also suggestive. Such openings are charted in figure 5, which indicates a division between a group consisting of Davies and Laurence and a group consisting of Atwood, Cohen, and Callaghan. The tendency towards left-branching — in other words, the tendency to begin sentences with participial clauses, subordinate adverbial clauses, and other adverbial elements — is one that is resisted by all three of the latter group. In this measure Atwood would seem at first glance to be less distinctive than she has appeared in others. But there are two additional considerations here. First, she is the most clausally complex writer of the five except for Davies, and if she were

FIGURE 4: LOCATION OF FIRST SUBORDINATOR AS RATIO OF DISTANCE BETWEEN STOPS

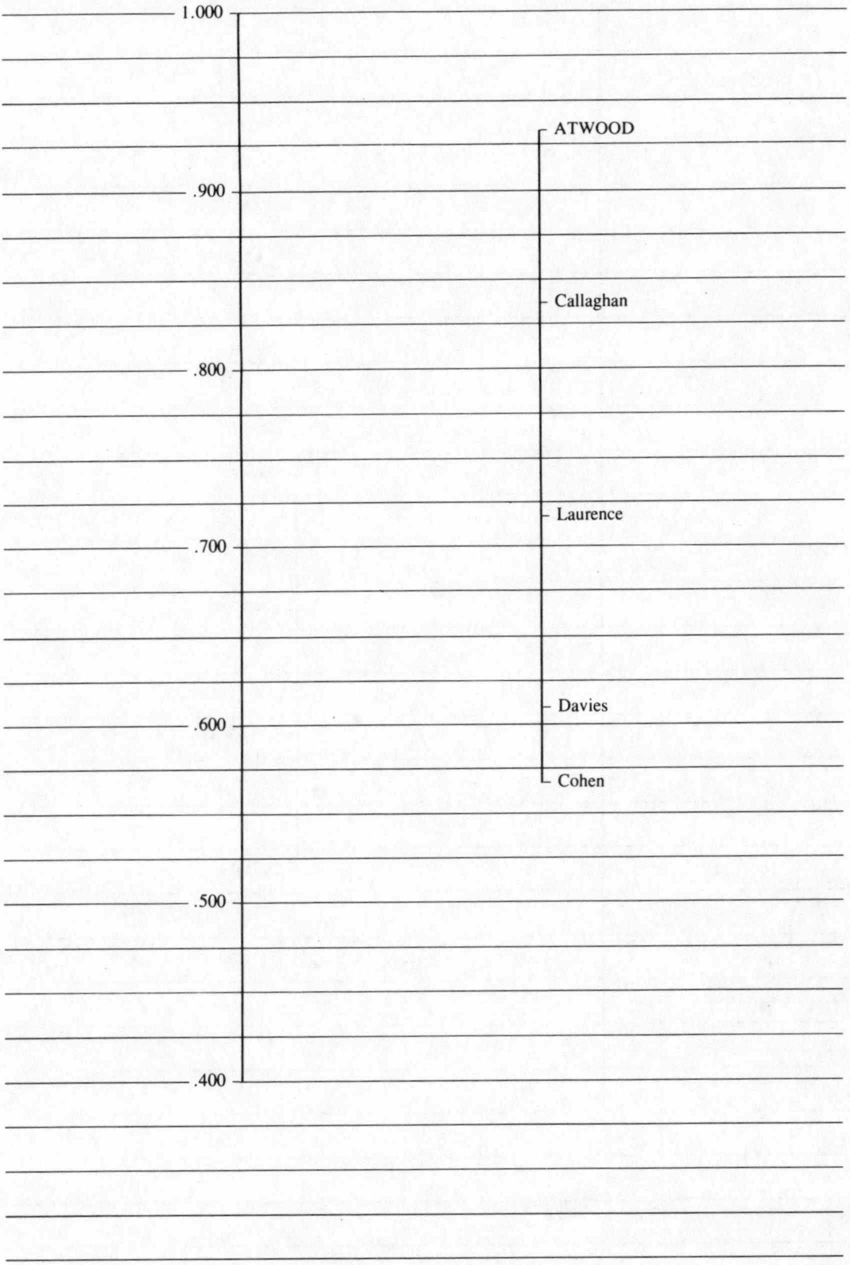

FIGURE 5: LEFT-BRANCHED SENTENCE OPENINGS

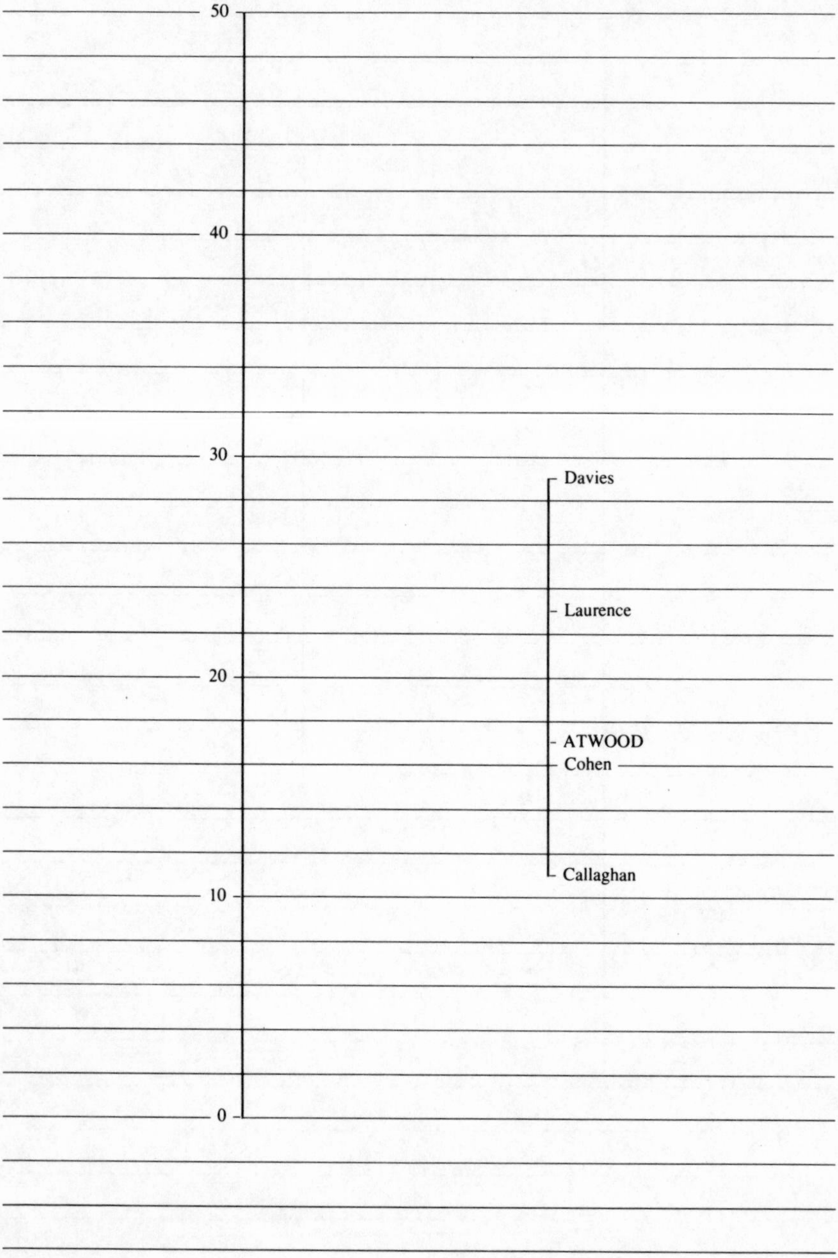

placing her subordinate and participial clauses normally, she would have more left-side subordinate clauses than any of the five except him. Since such clauses constitute the major part of left-branched openings, we should expect her to be in Laurence's place on the scale of figure 5 rather than where she is. Second, she has more locative elements in her sentence beginnings than either Cohen or Callaghan; hence, the density of what is normally at the beginning of a left-branched sentence — time, condition, and cause — is less in Atwood than in any other of the five. To illustrate: Callaghan is renowned for his endless parataxis, but he often will disrupt it with openings like the following:

> After an automobile ride one night he asked Vera . . . .
> Though making certain positive reservations she
>   felt herself . . . .
> Coming home from the yard at half past five o'clock
>   Harry smelled . . . .
> When she kissed him like that, closing her eyes,
>   he felt that he had not known her very long . . . . (9611, *Strange Fugitive*, pp. 10–11)

Cohen, too, will vary the pace of his short clauses with adverbials of several structural types:

> If there were Germans coming down the street . . . .
> When his father married he swore to kill any
>   man who . . . .
> While his father was gasping under the oxygen
>   tent . . . .
> Not long ago Breavman watched his mother read
>   the *Star*. (9613, *The Favorite Game*, pp. 16–17)

Three of Callaghan's four openings are temporal, one concessive; three of Cohen's four are temporal, one conditional. In Atwood, the pattern is far likelier to run as follows:

> On top was a layer of paperbacks . . . .
> Beside the larger eggs were smaller ones . . . .
> Behind me someone came into the room . . . . (9662, *Sfg*, pp. 90–91)

To be sure, there are temporal left-branches — even conditional ones — in the book, but the locative tendency is stronger in Atwood than in the others. It is a natural tendency, given the book's theme — not *whodunit* but "Where is he?" and, by resonant extension, "*Where* am I?" Except for the specifically *locative* left branches, the style is just as stripped of adverbial sentence openings as it is of all other devices of variation and colouring.

Figure 6 (total finite subordinate clauses, total rank-shifted clauses of all kinds) shows the extent to which Atwood can be considered a clausally complex writer, and it is considerable. A look at a few specific instances of her right-branching is illuminating:

Finally she had to back down: he could fight, but only *if* they hit first.

A mosquito lights on my arm and I let it bite me, *waiting* till its abdomen globes with blood before I pop it with my thumb like a grape.

I look around at the walls, the window; it's the same, it hasn't changed, but the shapes are inaccurate *as though* everything has warped slightly. (9662, *Sfg*, pp. 72-73, emphasis added)

The monotone of short independent clauses is relieved somewhat by the rank-shifted clauses that begin with the italicized words. The basic strategy of sentence design illustrated above prevails throughout the book: the weight of things is placed heavily on the right-hand side.

A final feature of *Surfacing's* habitual structure of finite clauses is predicator placement. Figure 7 displays a number of word-class sequences that are *prima facie* evidence of minimum fetch betweeen the predicator and the head of the subject phrase (for example, determiner-noun-verb, "The dog barked," determiner-noun-auxiliary "The house will," and pronoun-auxiliary verb, "He has gone"). Things like these are evidences of what we might call direct predication. Atwood outdistances all of the others, a mark not only of her disinclination to embed adverbial elements medially but also of her insistent right-branching sentence development.

PHRASES

A similar tendency is evident in Atwood's phrase-building. As is shown in figure 8, Atwood, to an extent that doubles the average of the controls, has a strong propensity for apposition and post-modifying adjectives, in other words for what might be called right-branching noun phrases. A few examples will suffice:

FIGURE 6:

TOTAL FINITE SUBORDINATE CLAUSES/TOTAL RANK-SHIFTED CLAUSES OF ALL KINDS

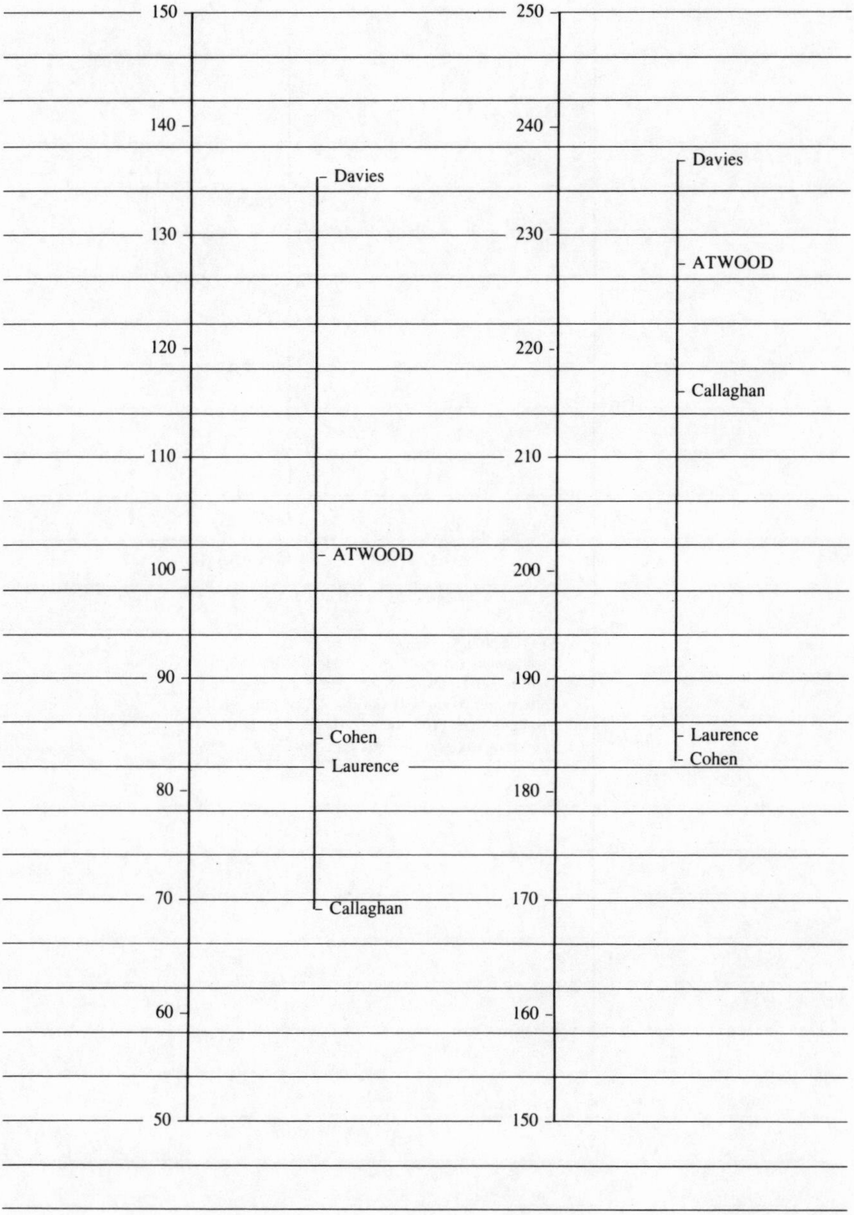

FIGURE 7: DIRECT PREDICATION

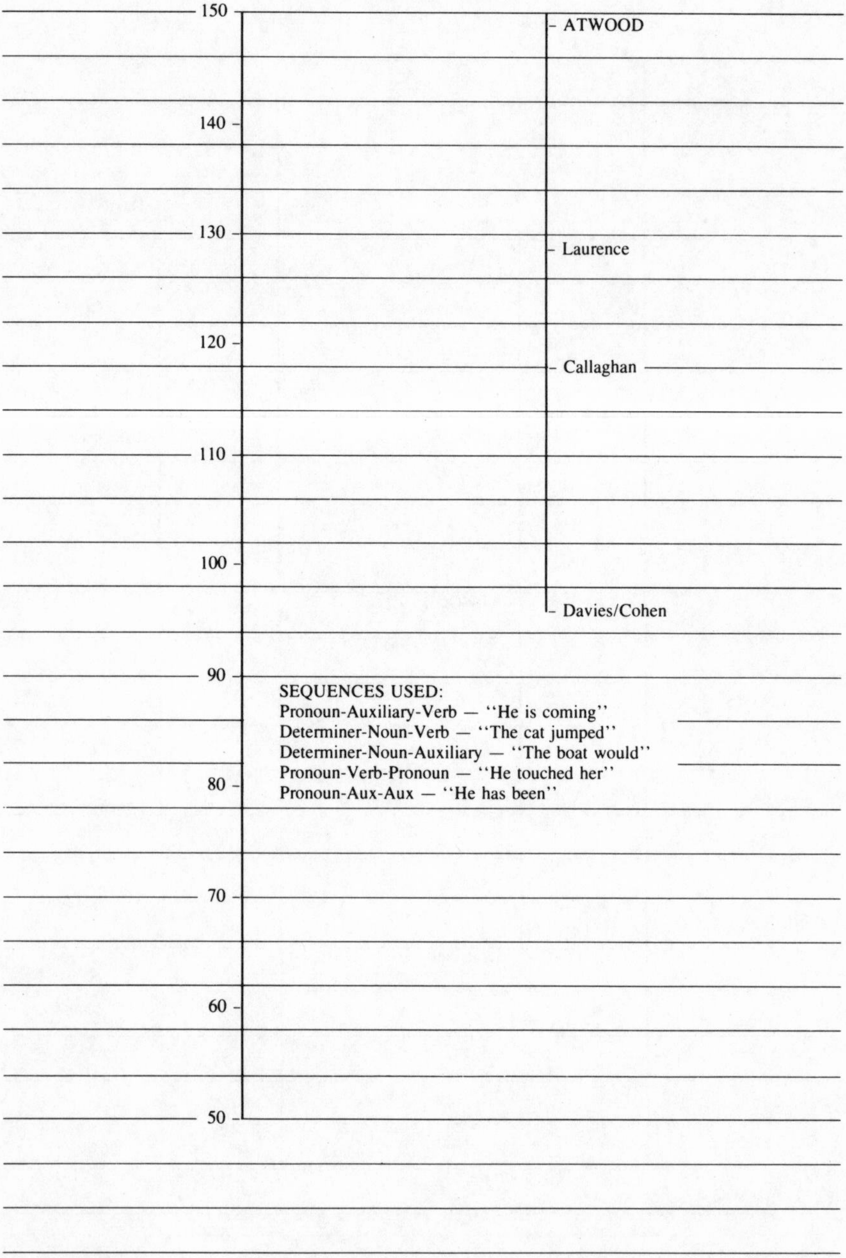

```
150 ─┬─────────────────────────── ATWOOD

140 ─

130 ─────────────────────────── Laurence

120 ─

                              ─ Callaghan ───────────

110 ─

100 ─

                              ─ Davies/Cohen

 90 ─
      SEQUENCES USED:
      Pronoun-Auxiliary-Verb — "He is coming"
      Determiner-Noun-Verb — "The cat jumped"
      Determiner-Noun-Auxiliary — "The boat would"
      Pronoun-Verb-Pronoun — "He touched her"
 80 ─  Pronoun-Aux-Aux — "He has been"

 70 ─

 60 ─

 50 ─┴───────────────────────────
```

FIGURE 8: APPOSITION and POSTMODIFYING ADJECTIVES

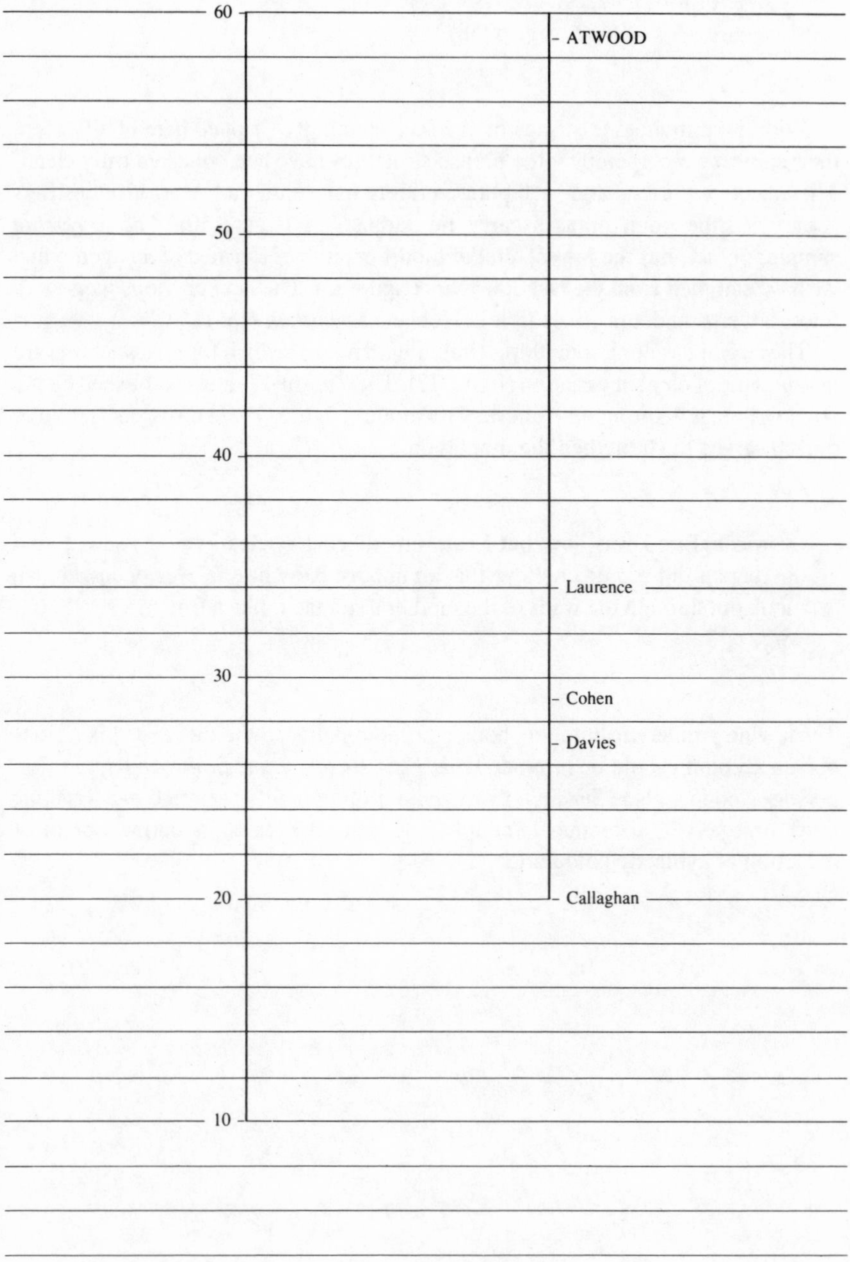

> The sound of love in the north, a *kiss*, a *slap*.
> We pass gigantic stumps, *level* and *saw-cut* . . . .
> I watch for the blazes, still *visible* after 14
>   years . . . . (9662, *Sfg*, p. 58)

Within the monotone strings of clauses, seemingly stripped bare of all except their subject-verb openings, the phrase structures have been plucked truly clean. The adjective phrases and verb phrases rarely have either adverbs or intensifiers (figure 9), the noun phrases carry few adjectives (figure 10). The *Surfacing* sample, in fact, has the lowest total of modifiers in it of *any* text of *any* genre that we have sampled from the last 300 years (figure 11). The next previous work with fewer adverbs and adjectives in it is Hobbes' *Leviathan* (1651).[6]

The author has done something similar with nouns, which for many authors are instruments of elegant variation (figure 12). The "normal" ratio established by the other writers is 48 pronouns for every 100 nouns (figures 12, 13); Atwood's ratio of 66:100 serves to strengthen the monotone:

> It was before I was born but I can remember it as clearly as if I saw it, and perhaps I did see it: I believe that an unborn baby has its eyes open and can look out through the walls of the mother's stomach, like a frog in a jar. (9662, *Sfg*, p. 32)

Those who would attribute this book's pronominality to the fact that it is a first-person account should be reminded that *Fifth Business* and *Stone Angel*, are first person accounts also. *Surfacing's extreme* pronominality, extreme even against other first-person accounts, is simply one more aspect of its entire system of reduction of syntactic colouration.

FIGURE 9:

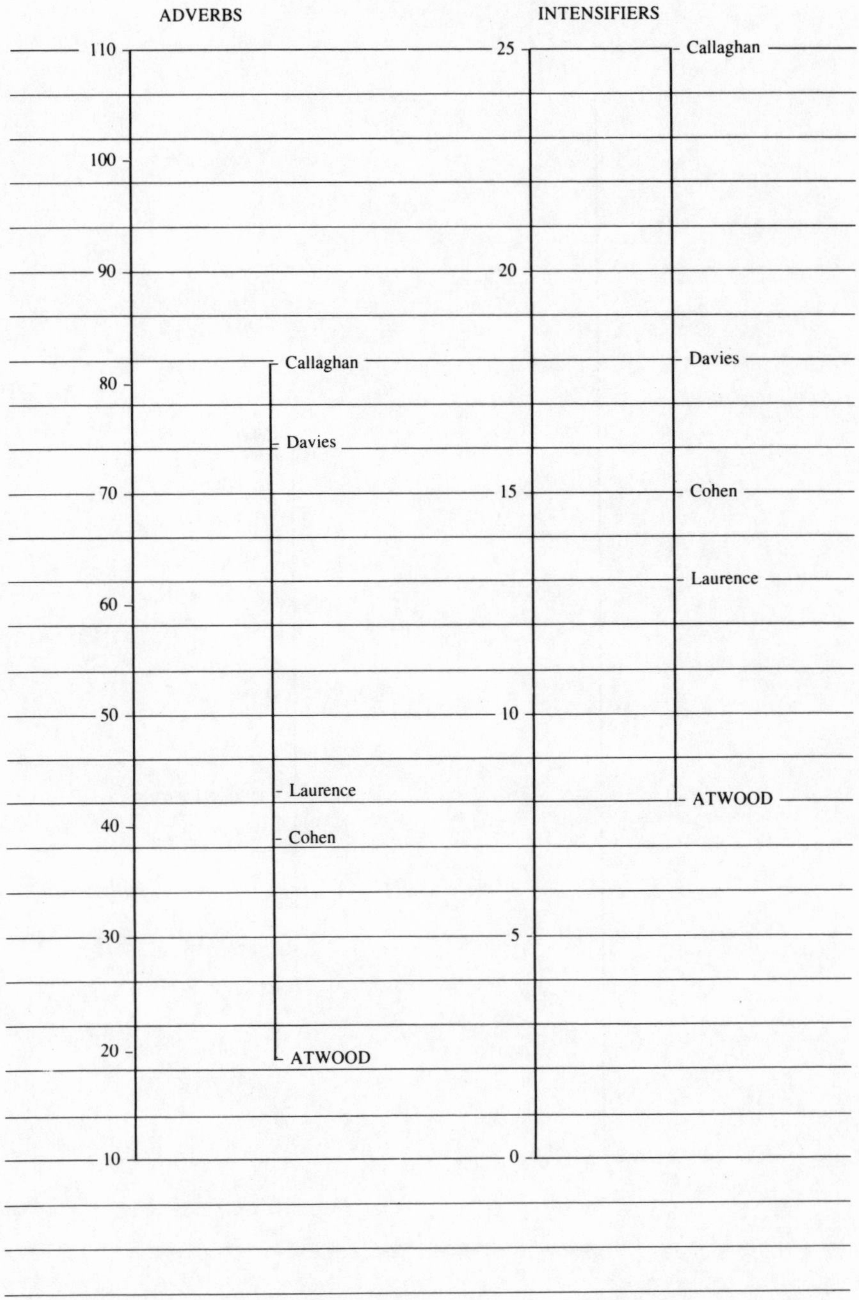
ADVERBS
INTENSIFIERS
110
100
90
80
70
60
50
40
30
20
10
25
20
15
10
5
0
Callaghan
Davies
Laurence
Cohen
ATWOOD
Callaghan
Davies
Cohen
Laurence
ATWOOD

FIGURE 10: ADJECTIVES

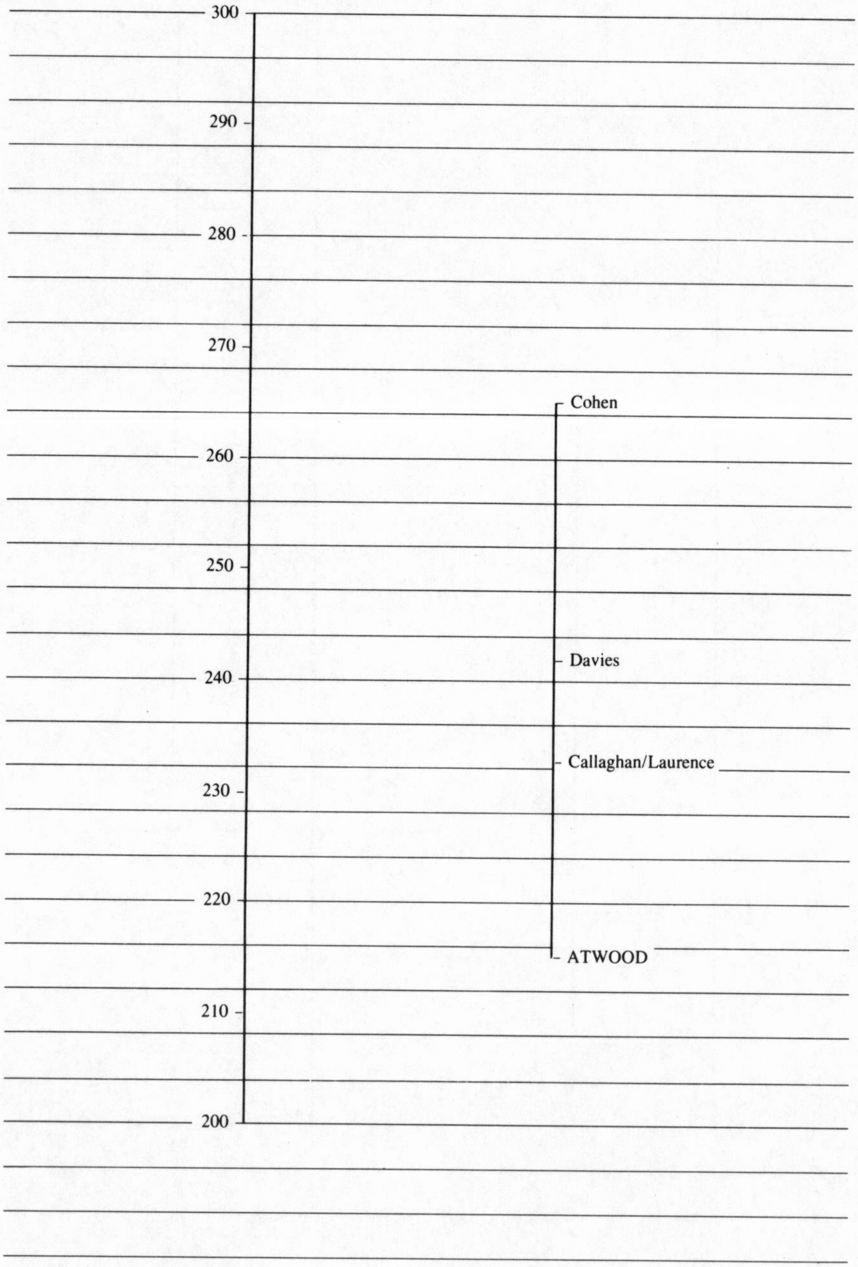

FIGURE 11: ''M'' STATISTIC: All Modifiers
(Adjective + Adverbs + Intensifiers + Function Adverbs)

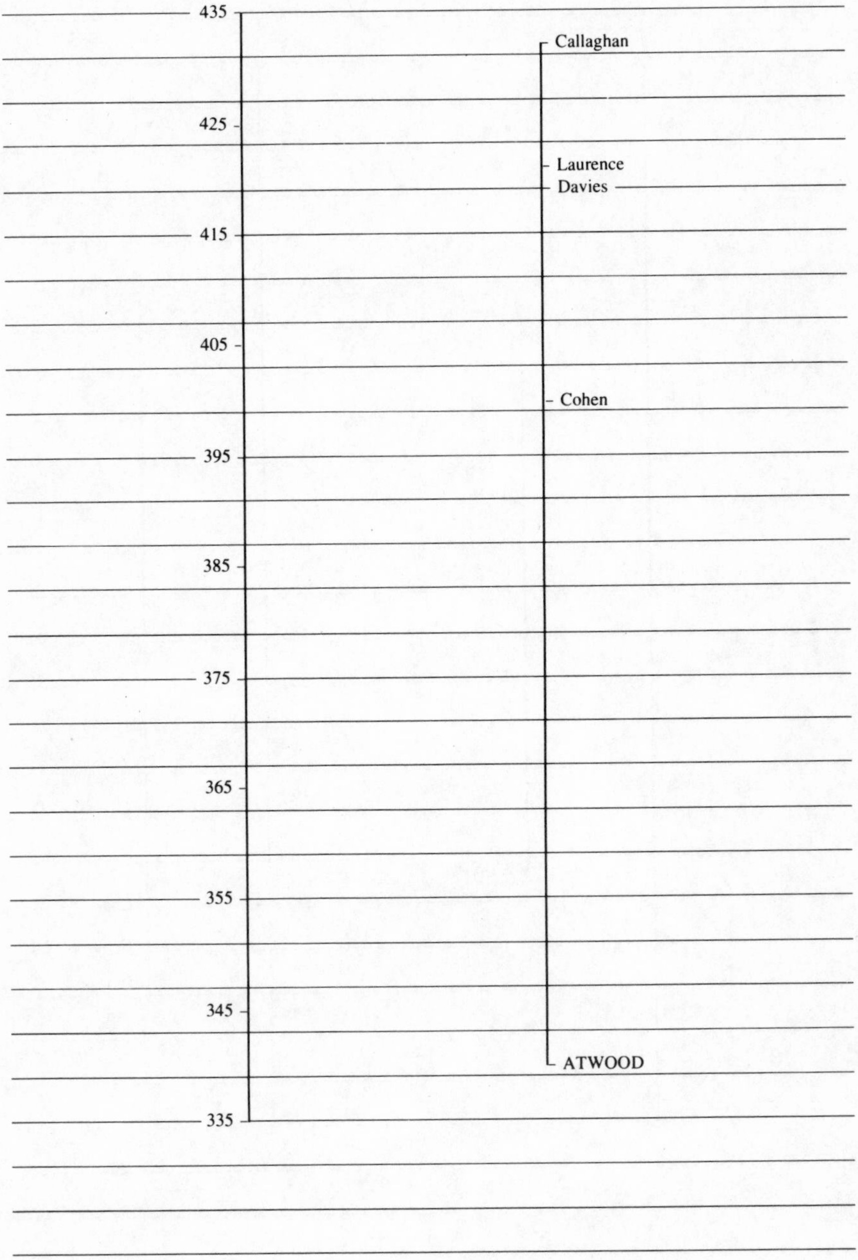

FIGURE 12

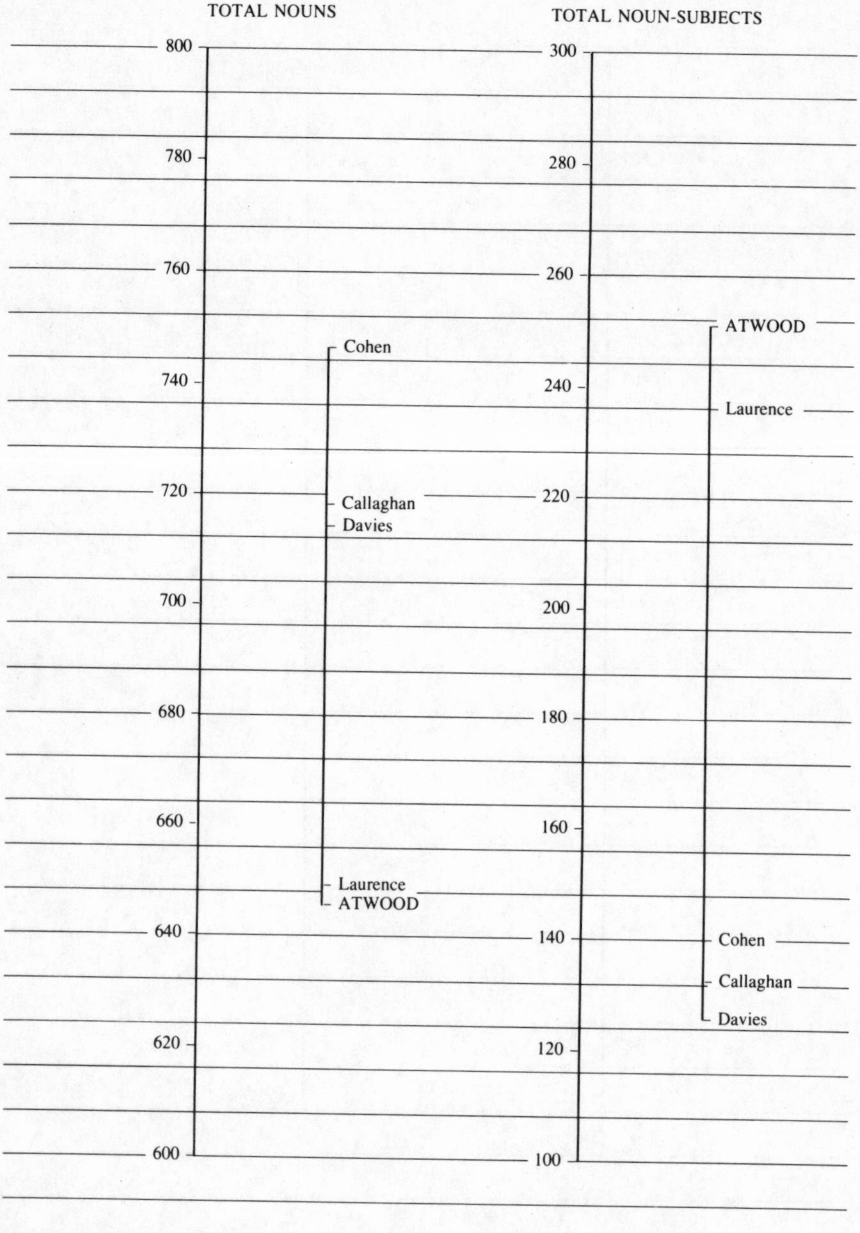
TOTAL NOUNS
TOTAL NOUN-SUBJECTS
800
780
760
740
720
700
680
660
640
620
600
Cohen
Callaghan
Davies
Laurence
ATWOOD
300
280
260
240
220
200
180
160
140
120
100
ATWOOD
Laurence
Cohen
Callaghan
Davies

FIGURE 13:

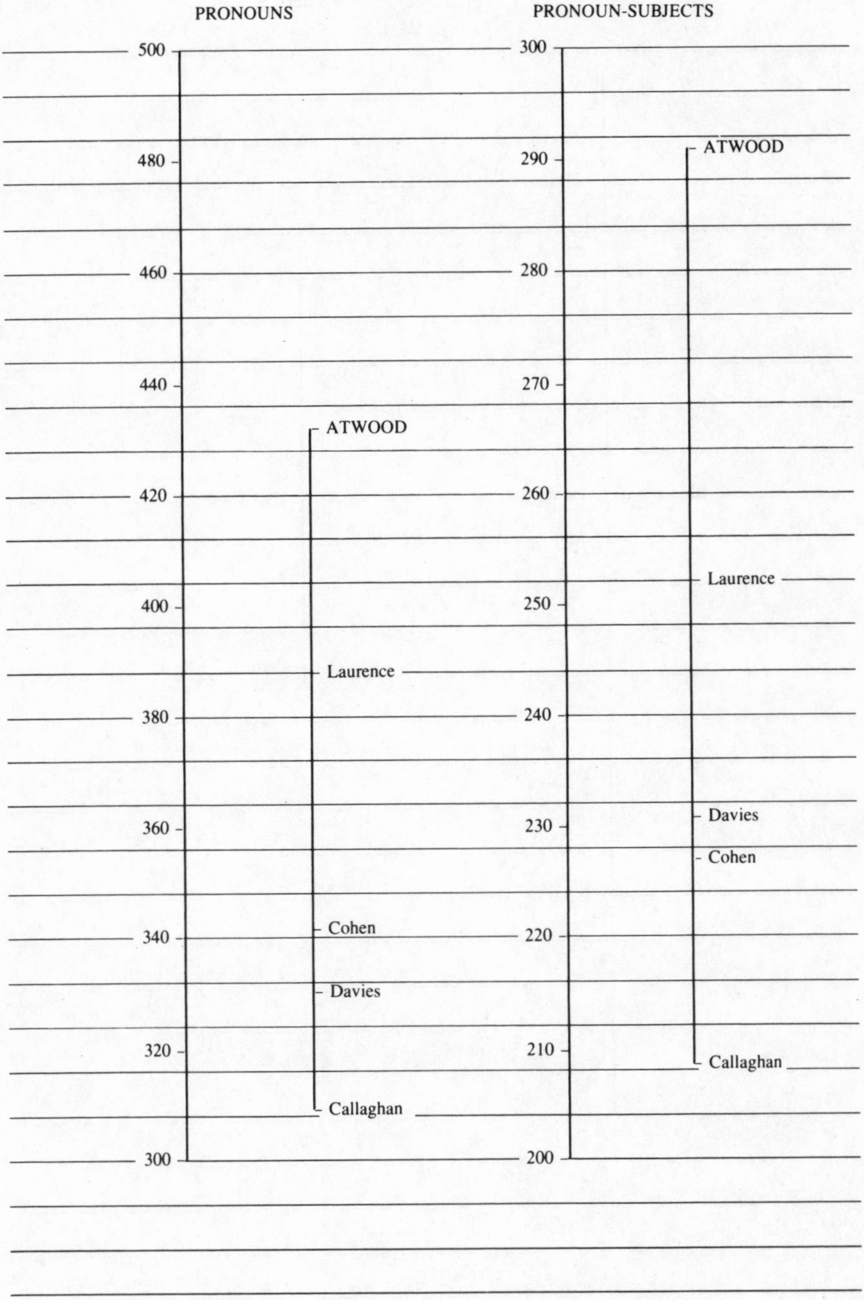

PRONOUNS	PRONOUN-SUBJECTS

PRONOUNS scale (left):
- 500
- 480
- 460
- 440
- ATWOOD (≈430)
- 420
- 400
- Laurence (≈385)
- 380
- 360
- 340 — Cohen
- Davies (≈330)
- 320
- Callaghan (≈310)
- 300

PRONOUN-SUBJECTS scale (right):
- 300
- ATWOOD (≈292)
- 290
- 280
- 270
- Laurence (≈253)
- 250
- 240
- Davies (≈232)
- 230 — Cohen (≈228)
- 220
- 210
- Callaghan (≈208)
- 200

FIGURE 14: "D" STATISTIC

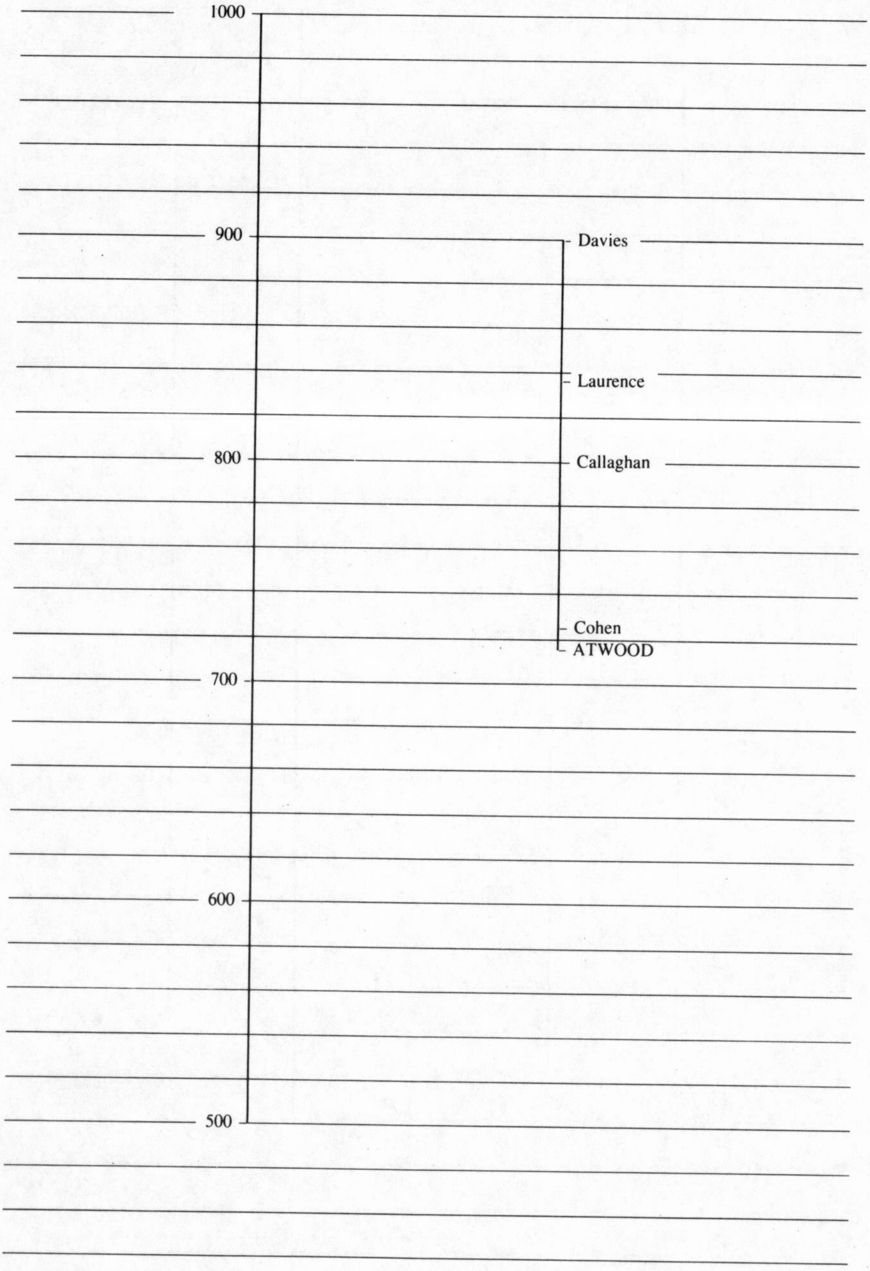

A further aspect of that system can be seen in a consideration of syntactic variety. The York Inventory's "D" statistic measures the extent to which a text exploits the range of word-class sequencing possible in English.[7] Average "D" values have declined over time as the language has become simpler — from an average "D" of 925 in the seventeenth century to an average of around 830 today. But around those averages there are startling exceptions: Ascham, Sidney, and Milton ran close to 1200, while the translators of the *Psalms* so sternly restricted their options as to produce the lowest "D" yet — 450 — a number almost matched by Gibbon's *Decline and Fall of the Roman Empire*. The "D" statistic of *Surfacing* (figure 14) is the lowest in the Inventory since Gibbon's autobiography.

CONCLUSIONS

Like other Atwood novels, *Surfacing* presents a crisis in the development of a female protagonist. Unlike the others, it involves a purifying passage through some kind of schizophrenic episode. (N.B., "Some of your lines are double," *Sfg*, p. 8.) That episode is marked geographically by a retreat into nearly untamed wilderness; it is marked in the heroine by her abandoning clothes, companions, and all other visible concomitants of civilization. The linguistic retrenchment that marks the book's syntax constitutes a similar retreat from ornate "civilized" values.

There is also the business of both clausal and phrasal right-branching — the apposition, the postmodification, the tendency to use subordinate clauses in situations where they will terminate rather than begin a sentence. Just as the novel itself embodies a process of discovery, so do the surface structures of its syntax. Things are not named; they are discovered, discovered even in parataxis:

> The forest thickens and I watch for the blazes, still visible after fourteen years; the trees they've cut on have grown swollen edges around the wounds, scar tissue. (9662, *Sfg*, p. 46)

It is difficult, in connection with the book's extraordinary appositional quality, not to think of *Heart of Darkness*, another journey into self-discovery in which a similar syntactic strategy is similarly foregrounded.

A final interesting point is that to the naked eye the style of *Surfacing* is different from the styles of all of Atwood's other novels. Not just different — radically different. On a reading of the others I would expect computerized syntactic data to reflect numerical differences of a magnitude unseen within the corpus of any writer since Thomas Carlyle.[8] This, of course, is mere speculation. But if, as I suspect it is accurate speculation, then in *Surfacing* Atwood might well have given us a *tour de force* richer at its most subtle levels than anyone has yet dared to imagine.

TABLE 1: SUMMARY OF SYNTACTIC ARRAYS
FROM FIGURES 1 TO 8 AND 11

Figures	Atwood 9662	Callaghan 9611	Cohen 9613	Davies 9615	Laurence 9618
1. Full and Half Stops	272	195	256	151	244
2. Average Clause Interval —					
finite only	7.54	7.91	7.84	8.58	7.45
In words — all clauses	5.84	5.88	6.36	6.85	6.05
3. Subject-Minus Coordinated					
Clauses	42	82	53	62	84
4. Location of First Subordinator					
As Ratio of Distance					
Between Stops	.940	.840	.570	.610	.720
5. Left-Branched Sentence					
Openings	17	11	16	29	23
6. Total Finite Subordinate					
Clauses/	101	65	85	135	82
Total Rank-Shifted Clauses of					
all Kinds	228	215	182	257	185
7. Direct Predication	149	118	96	96	128
8. Apposition and Postmodifying					
Adjectives	59	20	29	27	34
11. "M" Statistic: All Modifiers					
(Adjectives + Adverbs + Intensifiers + Function Adverbs)	340	433	400	419	421

TABLE 2: SUMMARY OF WORD-CLASS
DISTRIBUTIONS FROM FIGURES 9, 10, 12 AND 13

		Atwood 9662	Callaghan 9611	Cohen 9613	Davies 9615	Laurence 9618
01	Noun	646/19.6%	717/21.2%	747/22.5%	715/21.0%	649/19.3%
02	Verb	337/10.2	375/11.1	341/10.3	300/ 8.8	368/11.0
03	Descriptive Adjective	215/ 6.5	232/ 6.9	264/ 7.9	242/ 7.0	232/ 6.9
04	Descriptive Adverb	19/ 0.6	81/ 2.4	39/ 1.2	74/ 2.2	43/ 1.3
05	Infinitive	43/ 1.3	33/ 1.0	42/ 1.3	43/ 1.3	31/ 0.9
06	Participle	75/ 2.3	97/ 2.9	45/ 1.3	36/ 1.1	56/ 1.7
07	Gerund	9/ .3	21/ .6	13/ .4	22/ 0.6	16/ 0.5
11	Pronoun	433/13.3	309/ 9.2	341/10.3	331/ 9.7	384/11.4
21	Auxiliary Verb	280/ 8.5	169/ 5.0	216/ 6.5	250/ 7.3	283/ 8.4
31	Determiner	418/12.7	467/13.8	461/13.9	426/12.5	383/11.4
32	Postposition	27/ .8	52/ 1.5	24/ .7	20/ 0.6	43/ 1.3
33	Intensifier	8/ .2	25/ .7	15/ .5	18/ 0.5	13/ .5
34	Function Adverb	97/ 2.9	94/ 2.8	81/ 2.4	81/ 2.6	137/ 4.1
42	Subordinator	62/ 1.9	52/ 1.5	52/ 1.6	87/ 2.6	57/ 1.7
43	Relative	29/ .9	13/ .4	33/ 1.0	48/ 1.4	25/ .7
51	True Preposition	330/10.0	351/10.4	356/10.7	379/11.1	308/ 9.2
61	Pattern Marker	22/ .7	10/ .3	20/ .6	16/ 0.5	21/ .6
91	Sentence Corrector Intra sentence	4/ .1	6/ .2	2/ .6	7/ 0.2	5/ .2
98	Full Stop	132/ 4.0	3/ .1	5/ .2	24/ .7	9/ .3
99	Terminal Punctuation	140/24.8	192/17.7	251/13.4	127/27.3	235/14.5
015	Noun-Subject	104/ 3.2	133/ 3.9	145/ 4.4	105/ 3.1	116/ 3.5
115	Pronoun Subject	291/ 8.8	208/ 6.2	226/ 6.8	230/ 6.7	251/ 7.5
014	Predicate Noun	12/ .4	8/ .2	18/ .5	47/ 1.4	13/ .4
017	Appositive	38/ 1.2	6/ .2	7/ .2	14/ .4	18/ .5
213	be (main verb)	100/ 3.0	48/ 1.4	83/ 2.5	97/ 2.8	83/ 2.5

Notes

* The author wishes to thank Nancy Elizabeth Wright, who did a great deal of interpretive work on the data herein described, and Leslie Gaskin, who drew both the figures and the tables.

1. The process of sampling and the various manipulations of the programs are described in chapter 3 of my book, *Prose Style and Critical Reading* (N.Y.: Teachers College Press, Columbia University, 1976).
2. Subject-minus zeugmatic additioning is simply a grammarian's term for what our school teachers called a compound predicate with a single subject. For example, in "He went to the store and bought a shirt." the second clause (*and bought a shirt*) is a subject-minus zeugmatic additioning.
3. Davies' archaism is explored in my article, "Robertson Davies: The Tory Mode," *Journal of Canadian Studies* 12 (1977): 41–46.
4. A finite clause has a full-inflected verb in it — in other words a verb that is not a participle, gerund, or infinitive. These latter three are the mainsprings of what are called non-finite clauses.
5. The program shows how far (in words) the average distance from sentence beginning to point of first subordinate clause is. The average distance between stops is derived by dividing the total number of words in the sample by the total number of stops.
6. For a full history of the growth of the modifying words in literary prose since the 17th century, see *Prose Style and Critical Reading*, chapter 9.
7. The "D" statistic is specifically the measure of the number of *different* sequences of three word-classes present in a 3500 word text.
8. Carlyle is the only writer (of over 200) in the Inventory to date to be able to make a *major* alteration of his syntactic habits once launched on a professional writing career. Between *Schiller* and *Sartor Resartus*, his "D" Statistic, usually stable within 40 points over a writer's whole career, jumped by 250.

6

Surfacing:
Amerindian Themes and Shamanism

Marie-Françoise Guédon

The use of Indian elements identified as such in the text of *Surfacing* is restricted to a few local details and characters on one hand and to the mention of pictographs and some associated rituals on the other. Except for the pictographs, the use of local Indian themes is minimal and totally anecdotal. In spite of the ritual tone of the elements chosen, there is no attempt to work any Indian philosophy or cosmology into the perception of the human and natural environments or into the development of the novel as a whole. Neither the heroine nor the author makes any attempt to recreate or display an Indian perception of the world nor do the rare Indian characters. The setting is thoroughly modern and Euro-Canadian.

In this discussion I am limiting myself to those elements which are common to *Surfacing* and to North American Indian traditions, especially those which belonged to the cultures defining the people who live in the region where the action of the novel takes place. Within the context of these Indian themes, the nature of the vision quest and shamanic tradition will be considered as they apply to *Surfacing*.

Before going further, however, the remarkable diversity of the North American Indian cultures should be noted. It is difficult, if not impossible, to speak of "Indian" in general, especially when dealing with past traditions; therefore, I prefer to identify, whenever possible, the "Indian" people of the novel with the Algonkians, Cree, Ottawa, or Ojibwa Indian people who have actually lived in or near the geographical location of the story. This is not, however, a completely satisfying solution because the novel does not deal with the actual Indians of Ontario and Québec, but with the much less defined "Indian" people who inhabit the mind of the heroine. How closely the two categories fit together remains to be elucidated in the following pages, but it is possible to hypothesize an almost mythical dimension to the Indian elements chosen by Margaret Atwood.

Of the various Indian elements in *Surfacing*, the shamanic tone is the most fascinating and puzzling. Created through a remarkable and subtle play of pictures, animals, gestures, and scenes used as recurrent symbols throughout the book, this tone gives the central quest its shape and meaning. Some of the symbols have an Indian-resonant counterpart, but the shamanic system and the system born from and described in *Surfacing* lead in two very different directions.

I will be concerned here mostly with the second and last parts of the novel and will examine it without reference to other works by Atwood. All discussions will be centred on three areas: the Indian theme, the vision quest, and the shamanic tradition.

THE INDIAN THEME

The Indian theme in *Surfacing* intervenes directly through different motifs, the main ones being the pictographs and the figure which emerges from them, the ritual gestures and attitudes through which the heroine handles this new environment, the spirits or powers and their insertion in the human world, and the action itself — this quest for sanity which can be seen as a spirit quest and which may bring humans into contact with a part of the shamanic world. However, Atwood's skilful handling of the symbolic meaning carried by the term "Indian" should first be noted. There is no trace of association with the primitive aspect of the human; rather, the novel implies that in its traditional or mythical sense that which is "Indian" is definitely not part of the modern world. This convention opens the symbolic field by letting the Indian theme carry the hint of possible contacts with the non-human world which, in turn, will give access to "truth" and reality.

The rituals presented in the novel themselves carry specific connotations. Not identified as Indian, they simply and directly derive from the relationship of the heroine with her environment. From the freeing of the frog to the offering of clothing to the gods of the cliff to the taboos defining the world of power, all of these rituals express a recognition of and finally an acquaintance with the non-human world. They are the signs and means of the heroine's journey in a universe of non-human powers, of her progression toward dehumanization and of the necessary dive into the madness from which she regains her full reality.

Whether Margaret Atwood borrowed these rituals and beliefs (which are part of a stock of traditions shared by numerous peoples all over the Northern hemisphere) directly from Indian traditions or indirectly from her own childhood or even from the tales told by the early French or English Canadians, they constitute a link between the Euro-American cultures and the Amerindian tradition, and are for readers — as they become for the heroine — a doorway into the other world.

In keeping with the personal tone of *Surfacing* and with the heroine's character, the exact geographic location of the setting is not given, but the novel is set somewhere on the border between Ontario and Québec in one of those northern towns developed around the logging industry. The few Indians who are seen simply compose the background together with the other inhabitants of the town and village, the stores, and the buildings. They are the "others" (*Sfg*, p. 85) mentioned only in passing: the children on the roadside, the family crossing the lake during blueberry season long ago. A touch of mystery is attached to the coming and going of this small group "condensing as though from the air . . . and then disappearing . . . as though they had never been there" (*Sfg*, pp. 85-86), and to their survival in this alien world: "No one knew where they lived during the winter" (*Sfg*, p. 86). Indian people in general are finally more firmly, but also more vaguely, acknowledged — since it is without reference to individual characters — as the keepers of the powers represented by and embodied in the pictographs through which the heroine has first access to the reality she seeks.

The pictographs are interesting among other reasons because they belong to one of the cultural categories that even now defies exact attribution to a given location or culture. They cannot be dated with precision since for the most part they are drawn on vertical rocks or cliffs which cannot be worked into the usual archeological strata on which most dating methods are based. If the description of the pictographs given in the text is followed precisely, the figures would seem to fit the set of drawings found on the shores of the Great Lakes rather than in the Ontario-Québec border area where, as far as I know, antlered human or semi-human figures have not yet been found. They correspond to the Canadian Shield complex as a whole and to the Ojibwa and Cree traditions. Both Ojibwa and Cree, together with the Ottawa Indians, would have travelled to and lived in this area.

A clear intrusion of the native Indian tradition into the life of white people, the pictographs bear the double strength of the mystery usually attached to such prehistoric rock art and of their own design and symbolism. They are also a focus of supernatural, religious, or ceremonial significance. Finally, in the novel they play a major role by marking each step of the heroine's transformation, undergoing a parallel metamorphosis which brings them from crude drawings to living signs of sacred power while the heroine correspondingly moves from the dead illusion of a fake past to an unbroken reality.

For the North American Indian, each pictograph or symbol represented on a hide, stick, birch bark, or rock surface for other than purely decorative reasons (and there are very few instances of purely decorative Indian art) carries its own message. The North American Indian pictographs, defined by Selwyn Dewdney as "any example of the two dimensional art of a preliterate culture that is assumed to have a communicative (as distinct from a purely decorative) intent, whether at supernatural, shamanistic or secular levels,"[1] are neither graffiti nor political statements. The rock art of central and Eastern Canada is part of a traditional culture or set of cultures which assigned to each drawing a definite meaning. Ethnological studies of Algonkian Indian culture and especially of the Cree, Ojibwa, Ottawa, and Montagnais-Naskapi cultures, and the studies of pictographs in the Canadian Shield woodland area, have led to the recognition of definite connections between the ceremonial life of the Indians living in these areas and the designs executed with red ochre on the surfaces of outcroppings of rocks over-hanging rivers or lakes which can be reached only by canoe or boat. The research work done by Selwyn Dewdney and Kenneth E. Kidd is one of the best sources for information on the subject. They summarize their findings as follows:

> It is clear that the Indian occupation of the Canadian Shield country goes a long way back in time, and that there has been a succession of peoples living in it. That there was change and movement of group is certain . . . Those [rock paintings] now in existence are most likely the work of a people of Woodland culture, probably the Lake Woodland of prehistoric and Eastern Woodland of early historic times . . . The rock paintings still in existence indirectly mirror some aspects of their makers' attitudes to their external world and sometimes their thinking. They portray certain of their game animals, such as moose and bear; and the canoes and wigwams shown illustrate the world of their own creation. Over and above these aspects the paintings also illustrate some of the creatures of the native mind, in the shape of mythical or supernatural beings like the thunderbird, the serpent, the turtle, and the pipe-smoking moose.[2]

We know from the few Algonkian informants who can provide some information that the paintings are linked to shamanic practices and to dreams.

Of all the information available about the meaning of the figures painted on rocks, the most relevant concerns two beings particularly respected by the Ojibwa and Cree Indian people and connected with rocks: May-may-gway-shi, the rock fairy or rock spirit, or, in Dewdney's terms, the Rock medicine Man, and Mis-shi-pi-zhiw or Misshipeshu, the Great Lynx, also known as Water Panther, Snake Monster, Underwater Cat, or the Lion.

> The Ojibwa have a mischievous being called Maymaygwayshi, who lives in cracks and shallow caves along the water. He is very fond of fish and often robs the traps of the Indians. This spirit appears as a short, large-headed creature, sometimes with horns. The Ojibwa shaman was supposed to have the power to enter rocks and trade tobacco with the spirit for "rock medi-cine."[3]

The Great Lynx or water monster often looks like or is identified with a horned snake. Selwyn Dewdney describes it as follows:

Mishipizhiw is a supernatural creature, highly dangerous, who inhabits the rapids on some streams . . . He appears in some of the bark rolls as a cat-like creature with large ears or horns and a long tail. So frequent a motif did he become in Ojibwa art that he is sometimes depicted on their woven bags . . . John Turner . . . an early author who lived most of his life among the Ojibwa, illustrated the Great Lynx as a cat-like creature with spiny back . . . It is worthy of note here that in the bark rolls, lines radiating from a figure of a man or an animal are meant to imply "power" in that figure; hence the spines on the back of the Great Lynx may be a device for emphasizing his great supernatural power.[4]

Not a pleasant or a safe figure, Misshipeshu's enormous strength combined with cunning malevolence and the call of death all serve to evoke dread. It is this figure which Atwood, without identifying it, has chosen to project her heroine's fears and hope. In the translation process, Misshipeshu loses some satanic attributes, but its power remains present and its possibilities are exploited to the fullest. Looking through her father's papers, the narrator encounters Misshipeshu for the first time:

a crude drawing of a hand, done with a felt pen or a brush, and some notations: numbers, a name . . . More hands, then a stiff childish figure, faceless and minus the hands and feet, and on the next page a similar creature with two things like tree branches or antlers protruding from its head. (*Sfg*, p. 59)

Later she sees that its

body was long, a snake or a fish; it had four limbs or arms and a tail and on the head were two branched horns. Lengthwise it was like an animal, an alligator; upright it was more human, but only in the positions of the arms and the front-facing eyes. (*Sfg*, p. 101)

Such is the first meeting with the power which will lead her on her quest, and such is its first gift — meaning.

Atwood's heroine has glimpsed the true nature of the image, that it will become a guide for her. The scientific descriptions which follow are correct and carefully selected: "symbolic content, at the expense of expressiveness and form . . . [S]ites of the paintings are the abodes of powerful or protective spirits, which may explain the custom, persisting in remote areas, of leaving offerings of clothing and small bundles of 'prayer' sticks . . . [T]he paintings are associated with the practice of fasting to produce significant or predictive dreams . . . [R]ed among the Indians is a sacred colour" (*Sfg*, pp. 102–3). From this point on, these images are interiorized by the narrator, first when she dives near a cliff on the big lake (*Sfg*, p. 141) and later when the first part of the quest is fulfilled:

> It was there but it wasn't a painting, it wasn't on the rock. It was below me, drifting towards me from the furthest level where there was no life, a dark oval trailing limbs. It was blurred but it had eyes, they were open, it was something I knew about, a dead thing, it was dead. (*Sfg*, p. 142)

With it, the heroine finds her memory, the dead part of herself, her dead child. Her perception of the pictographs moves towards a new recognition as well. They are not things; they are the signs and doorways to salvation, to true vision. Her father "had discovered new places, new oracles, they were things he was seeing the way I had seen, true vision; at the end, after the failure of logic" (*Sfg*, p. 145). This vision entails new privileges, duties, and obligations; the metamorphosis is going on, she is not completely human any more, and she foresees that her father, whatever he may be, is no longer human either. But Joe, her lover, who once looked almost animal, appears now as a human. Contact with him can only be allowed under certain conditions: it would be a sacrilege to allow intimacy between a human, one of the killers of animals, and someone who is now part animal. Henceforward, the horned being takes on a fuller reality for the narrator. Its sacred nature is reaffirmed as one of the gods on the shore or in the water who has accepted her call for help. But it is also identified with her dead child, the aborted foetus which emerges from a complex memory. She now knows that she dealt with guilt and mutilation by fabricating a false reality which has prevented her from being complete until this point. Her own mystery is solved, but this is only the first step. She must prepare herself for the next one, for the god will return, anew, transformed, like the new embryo she must conceive, a god with shining fur, at once human and animal, "the first one, the first true human: (*Sfg*, p. 191).

The final apparition of the horned god summarizes the Indian theme as it announces the completion of the cycle, the return to ordinary reality. It draws together not only the various manifestations of the power in its sacred forms but also its most trivial aspects, such as the crudely carved wooden trout supporting the bar in the cheap motel where the narrator stopped at the beginning of her trip.

> From the lake a fish jumps
> An idea of a fish jumps
> A fish jumps, carved wooden fish with dots painted on the sides, no, antlered fish thing drawn in red on cliffstone, protecting spirit. It hangs in the air suspended, flesh turned to icon, he has changed again, returned to the water. How many shapes can he take.
> I watch it for an hour or so; then it drops and softens, the circles widen, it becomes an ordinary fish again. (*Sfg*, p. 187)

This endless chain of transformation recalls the ability to change shape, as much a gift of vision as it is a sign of power, often attributed to the medicine man or woman. That there is danger in the figure is clearly indicated in the heroine's last meeting with her father when she encounters "what my father saw, the thing you meet when you've stayed here too long alone" (*Sfg*, pp. 186–87). Such a transformation is the other side of the flow of life contained in the image of the fish which leads also to a return to the normal world. But before this last metamorphosis takes place, we meet the god in its Christian form, seen through the eyes of the little girl the narrator once was. She and her brother had "learned in the winter about the Devil and God: if the Devil was allowed a tail and horns, God needed them also, they were advantages" (*Sfg*, p. 158). This figure is part of the heroine's drawing in a scrapbook which her mother had kept. As the pictographs came from her father, so this picture is given back by her mother.

The next stage of the journey may now begin. The action to be taken is clearly indicated: the narrator must reassert the life she once took, must let the god be conceived in her. At this point it is interesting to note the convergence between Atwood's treatment of motherhood and womanhood in general and Indian beliefs on these subjects. In most North American Indian populations women from puberty to menopause are subject to a number of taboos which are especially strong during menstruation and many of which are oriented primarily toward the protection of future infants. During their menstruation, women are supposedly endowed with certain powers conflicting with the interest or even the safety of hunters and warriors. Menstrual blood is thought to attract wild animals and uncontrolled forces. Pregnant women have to respect avoidance rules protecting the unborn infant and its weak soul from the strong spirits of the animal world, which may be why the mother avoids freshly killed meat and fish. The infant is considered a being who is not yet fully human, who is still in contact with the non-human world of animals, spirits, and other powers. The infant may therefore still feel the call of that other world and has to be prevented from being pulled back toward it. One of the consequences of these beliefs is that new-born infants, pregnant women, and menstruating women are seen as loci or channels for such powers. Some of the taboos can be interpreted as protecting not the child but the community from the mother and child.

In such a context, the concept of a newly conceived infant as a sacred being, a god, an animal, is totally acceptable. When the heroine perceives the embryo as a "plant-animal" sending filaments into her as the furry god himself feeding on her, and finally as the "time-traveller, the primaeval one . . . the first true human" (*Sfg*, p. 191), she is acting in continuity with an old tradition. She recognizes the power of life and the special status of those who have just been in contact with its source.

It is, however, in the development of the theme of power and the meaning given to the term itself that Margaret Atwood draws nearer to the Ojibwa-Cree-Ottawa

Indian concept. Among most North American Indians, the notion of power derives from the consideration that every living being is not only a body but also a soul. According to the anthropologist Irving Hallowell, the "ultimate goal" of such a living being is "what the Ojibwa call *pímáda zíwin:* life in the most inclusive sense . . . [In this quest] the help of other selves — entities that are willing to share their power with men — is . . . most important. These [helpers] are the *pawáganak*."[5] Hallowell defines the *pawáganak* or "dream visitors" in terms that apply equally in most other Algonkian contexts:

> To the Ojibwa, then, human beings . . . i.e., Ojibwa Indians, are only one class of persons. The other class of persons, I believe, it is preferable to characterize as "other-than-human-beings," rather than supernatural beings, since their essential properties as persons are essentially the same. While they do not differ from human beings in kind, other-than-human persons occupy the top rank in the power hierarchy of animate beings. Metamorphosis is more characteristic of them, than of human beings.
>
> This second class of persons includes the four Winds, Sun and Moon, Thunderbirds, the "owners" or "masters" of the various species of plants and animals, and the characters in myths . . . .
>
> [They] are expected to share their knowledge and power with human beings . . . It is particularly important that men obtain "blessings" from [them] . . . that is the purpose of the aboriginal puberty fast, in which boys come "face to face" with other-than-human persons (*pawáganak*) in dreams or visions.[6]

Power, then, in Algonkian terms, is personalized and linked to animals, the dead, spirits, and other entities which are often supposed to be stronger than the human being who is granted some help from them. Hence, there is danger in handling a power without adequate protection or orientation. Power lets itself be recognized through signals that are subtle, hidden in the daily noise but nevertheless precise for those who are listening to its clues. It results in personal, physical, or mental strengths as well as in special gifts such as the ability to communicate with other beings, human or non-human, or the ability to *see* in the full sense of the word: to find lost objects, detect the truth of a statement, or acquire visionary powers.

Since the quest of Atwood's heroine is both a quest for power and one led by the powers she has met or summoned, her progression can be charted by identifying the changes in her conception and perception of that new world where power is at once a call, a beacon, and a helper. The first sign given is the recognition of the presence of power. In the beginning, power is still viewed as something to be avoided. Considering the old garden, the heroine reflects on some childhood memories:

The beans that were left too long would yellow after the first frost and split open. Inside were pebbles, purple-black and frightening. I knew that if I could get some of them and keep them for myself I would be all-powerful; but later when I was tall enough and could finally reach to pick them it didn't work. Just as well, I think, as I had no idea what I would do with the power once I got it; if I'd turned out like the others with power I would have been evil. (*Sfg*, p. 37)

It is only with the dive into the lake, searching for the pictographs, the dive into the irrational, that power appears undisguised, a gift from her dead father, from her dead child, and from the horned water god. It manifests itself immediately through her new awareness. When she meets Joe, her lover, the heroine realizes her distance from him: "I was wishing I could tell him how to change so he could get there, the place where I was" (*Sfg*, p. 146), and yet when Joe insists on making love, she sees his entrance into her body as a sacrilege which she cannot allow. What could be described as a shock leading to insanity is here very simply presented as a meeting with power which is directly translated into transformation. As in shamanic tradition, there is no power without metamorphosis.

When she returns to the cabin, it looks "different, larger, as though [she] hadn't been there for a long time," and she explains: "the half of me that had begun to return was not yet used to it" (*Sfg*, p. 148). English has become for her a foreign language with "imported" (*Sfg*, p. 150) words. She is also now aware of new dangers and possibilities. She watches fisherman approaching in their boat and knows that she has endured "the power" only because her "father had left [her] the guides, the man-animals and the maze of numbers" (*Sfg*, p. 149), but having obtained power and knowledge from her father, she must seek to be 'complete.' For this she must go to her mother to acquire guidance toward action.

The next stage of the quest begins with the surging of power from the guides. She learns to recognize when power is decreasing for it can be drawn away by contacts with the wrong person or the wrong object. As in the world of the Indian hunter or seeker, purity becomes a necessity — keeping away from those who cannot see, who lie: "the animals don't lie" (*Sfg*, p. 153). When Anna remarks, "God, she really is inhuman" (*Sfg*, p. 154), no one realizes how close the statement is to the truth. And when the narrator declines David's proposition, telling him she would get pregnant, and he protests ("You're putting me on . . . this is the twentieth century"), she can truthfully answer, "No it isn't . . . Not here" (*Sfg*, p. 151). Both geographically and psychologically, she has already stepped out of the modern human world.

As she proceeds, the power becomes more and more obvious. New insights are affirmed. When she looks at David, "The power flowed into my eyes, I could see into him, he was an imposter, a pastiche" (*Sfg*, p. 152). And when she watches a mushroom, "It sprang up from the earth, pure joy, pure death, burning white like snow" (*Sfg*, p. 150), and she experiences her capacity to *see*. Keeping away from human beings, she lets herself be led to her mother's gift, the scrapbook. With the power now in her, she is aware of moon and sun, leaves, rock, and water. She leads Joe (who is unaware of the context) outside and renews the life of her lost child. The new baby, conceived amidst such powers, is almost animal.

> [Joe] trembles and then I can feel my lost child surfacing within me, forgiving me, rising from the lake where it has been prisoned for so long, its eyes and teeth phosphorescent; the two halves clasp, interlocking like fingers, it buds, it sends out fronds. This time I will do it by myself, squatting, on old newspapers in a corner alone; or on leaves, dry leaves, a heap of them, that's cleaner. The baby will slip out easily as an egg, a kitten, and I'll lick it off and bite the cord, the blood returning to the ground where it belongs; the moon will be full, pulling. In the morning I will be able to see it: it will be covered with shining fur, a god, I will never teach it any words. (*Sfg*, pp. 161–62)

This extraordinary paragraph marks the climax of the journey but does not conclude it. In order to complete her quest, the heroine must confront herself and discover her own strength, but at this point the guiding powers seem to abandon her. This is a test of both her willingness and her ability to recognize the different manifestations of the powers, their coming and going becoming ever clearer signals. When the power "has drained away," when her "fingers are empty as gloves, eyes ordinary" (*Sfg*, p. 171), she comes to see the cabin as a refuge from the assaults of something or somebody she cannot control. Power is now a force external to her. But as she confronts her fear, it is precisely the fear itself which manifests the source of the power: what her parents have become.

> In the middle of the night silence wakes me, the rain has stopped. Blank dark, I can see nothing, I try to move my hands but I can't. The fear arrives like waves, like footfalls, it has no center; it encloses me like armour, it's my skin that is afraid, rigid. They want to get in, they want me to open the windows, the door, they can't do it by themselves. I'm the only one, they are depending on me but I don't know any longer who they are; however they come back they won't be the same, they will have changed. I willed it, I called to them, that they should arrive is logical; but logic is a wall, I built it, on the other side is terror. (*Sfg*, p. 174)

Once re-internalized, the fear becomes a guide, an immediate expression of the power and of its intent. She comes to know that "There must be rules: places I'm permitted to be, other places I'm not. I'll have to listen carefully, if I trust them they will tell me what is allowed" (*Sfg*, pp. 175-76). It is then that she meets the tradition of the Algonkian shaman, the initiate or dreamer for whom communication with other living beings is most intimate and is carried by feelings and intuitions as well as by images and words.

THE VISION QUEST

For the North American Indian cultures, as for most cultures with a hunting and gathering subsistence technology, nature is at once part of the human mind and a personalized fraction of the universe. It should be emphasized that among many cultures, and among North American Indian ones especially, most methods devised, for religious purposes among others, to dissociate the human individual from his socio-cultural environment involve a re-acquaintance with the world of animals, rocks, waters, skies, and other components of what we call the natural environment. It is through such meetings that "imaginary" powers and other spirits are evoked, contacted, accepted, and incorporated into the human psyche, informing the soul and its reality.

According to the vision of Atwood's heroine, nature is a complex concept which is remarkable because it allies some of the pervasive myths of our time with Amerindian-like archetypes. On one hand, nature is opposed to both the human and the modern world, contrapuntally set against the urban mechanized environment and the "Americans," those mechanized humans. On the other hand, contrary to its occidental definition and closer to its Algonkian counterpart, nature here includes, or at least implies the possibility of including, those human beings who are "true" or real. Moreover, it supposes a link with the supernatural world, communicating with animal and vegetable life. Ghosts belong to nature, and the unborn foetus still communes with the animal world.

The notion of a fundamental opposition betweeen nature and the technologically aggressive "Americans" has appeared in many guises in Western thought. Here it is expressed in the symbol of the heron:

> The shape of the heron flying above us the first evening we fished, legs and neck stretched, wings outspread, a bluegrey cross, and the other heron or was it the same one, hanging wrecked from the tree. Whether it died willingly, consented, whether Christ died willingly, anything that suffers and dies instead of us is Christ; if they didn't kill birds and fish they would have killed us. The animals die that we may live, they are substitute people, hunters in the fall killing the deer, that is Christ also. (*Sfg*, p. 140)

As described in this passage, the heron does not completely fit in the animal world and departs totally from the Ojibwa-Cree-Ottawa treatment of birds. Imaged primarily as a lynch victim which speaks against the "Americans" and accuses the city-machine world, the heron later takes on a fuller dimension and assumes its role of Christ-like victim. This last association is introduced by Atwood in order that the heroine may deal with the concept of guilt or sin, a concept alien to the Algonkian world.

For the Americans, as for David, the heron is only a trophy to suspend from a tree by a blue nylon rope or to capture inside a camera. As a living bird it cannot be "tamed or cooked or trained to talk, the only relation they could have to a thing like that was to destroy it" (*Sfg*, p. 116). But through the heron the narrator sees all of the other animals which modern human beings must not only kill to eat as in the past, but now needlessly destroy in the name of progress. Through their death she has access to all other needless deaths of trees, fish, frogs, and babies — as she is reminded by the mention of the frog which brings back the elusive memory of that part of herself which also died: "A part of the body, a dead animal. I wondered what part of them the heron was, that they needed so much to kill it" (*Sfg*, p. 119). The death of the heron also leads to the realization of the sin committed while fishing needlessly and to the heroine's first understanding of her special status: "I couldn't anymore, I had no right to" (*Sfg*, p. 120). The hidden metamorphosis has started, and the first move toward freedom is accomplished, a life-giving act. After watching a frog die as bait during a fishing trip, the heroine frees the frogs remaining in the jar, which brings back the two indissociable memories of her brother's collection of bottled frogs which died because she did not have the courage to free them and of the abortionist's table where her own child, another kind of bottled frog, died because she could not resist her first lover's will. Guilt is of course the immediate and common characteristic of the three events, with its overwhelming conclusion: "Because of my fear they were killed" (*Sfg*, p. 131). Because the same guilt is present everywhere in the human world, in adults as well as children, the return to childhood is not the way to redemption. The heroine has not yet regained the strength to act. She must somehow repair the desecration imposed on the heron, dissociate herself from it, before she can gain access to the gods hiding behind the animals and sustaining them.

For in *Surfacing* these gods are at the core of nature. Destroyed by the machines, they will survive as long as a tree, a mushroom, a frog, a heron survives. The animal powers or gods are the warrant and source of nature's sacredness. In the heroine's struggle to regain the lost part of herself there is more than an effort to recover from a personal crisis. She is attempting to renew contact with the original ground, with life itself. From her point of view, all modern human beings are separated from life by sins and lies, but nature cannot lie. It forces the human being thrust into its control to return to the truth. Hence the purification needed to meet it and brought by the meeting, for a special manner of seeing, truer than normal, is needed. The teaching or power of nature is not immediate. It passes through the "gods" who have to be perceived before they act; one has to submit to a quest which passes first through a revelation. One has to find certain keys; one has to go back to ancient doors. Nature, then, is a manner of seeing. Only as such does nature reveal its full power.

This full revelation involves an equally complete transformation of the seer. When it reaches this triumphant moment, the narrative is at once explicit and lyrical:

> Slowly I retrace the trail. Something has happened to my eyes, my feet are released, they alternate, several inches from the ground. I'm ice-clear, transparent, my bones and the child inside me showing through the green webs of my flesh, the ribs are shadows, the muscles jelly, the trees are like this too, they shimmer, their cores glow through the wood and bark.
>
> The forest leaps upward, enormous, the way it was before they cut it, columns of sunlight frozen; the boulders float, melt, everything is made of water, even the rocks. In one of the languages there are no nouns, only verbs held for a longer moment.
>
> The animals have no need for speech, why talk when you are a word
> I lean against a tree, I am a tree leaning
>
> (*Sfg*, p. 181)

The union can then be accomplished. Woman can merge with nature:

> I break out again into the bright sun and crumple, head against the ground
> I am not an animal or a tree, I am the thing in which the trees and animals move and grow, I am a place.
>
> (*Sfg*, p. 181)

There are several traits in this presentation which correspond to what is found in the Northern Algonkian cultures. However, the translation of Indian nature into Anglo-Saxon terms is hampered by a distinction which is widespread in the European world but unacceptable to the traditional Indian cosmologies: the opposition between natural and supernatural. In the Ojibwa-Cree-Indian world, continuity is expressed in the belief that although not everything is alive, many beings are considered alive which the Euro-Canadian culture has defined as inanimate. Spirits and animals belong to the same kingdom: the hunter kills the flesh of his game because he is in contact with its soul. But live beings are so because they have power. The boundary between animals — who, from the Ojibwa-Cree points of view, are endowed with a soul and power — and animal spirits is not only undefined but there is such a complementarity, a necessity for both ideas to be joined, that the concept of boundary is replaced by that of transformation. The same being may choose to present itself in different guises or may be seen from different angles according to the power of the beholder. In the Ojibwa-Cree world, every hunt is a ritual act. The meeting between the hunter and the game that will become meat is a meeting between two live individuals, two persons, and ultimately two souls, all levels being congruent.

Since not only the animals and plants, but also a number of natural features such as rivers, certain rocks, and elements such as rain, clouds and winds, are endowed with power, all are part of the same continuum, a society in which everyone — human and non-human — interacts with everyone else. To the perceiver every natural event may be, and is interpreted as, a personal message. This "society" reflects, or is reflected by, the human moral order. Animals and other non-human beings are sustained by the same values and drives as are essential to human lives. The natural world seems to be totally englobed by the supernatural world.

Yet the human world as such is distinguished from the non-human universe by limitations. Though man belongs to the same environment, he does not have ready access to all of it, and certainly not to most of the invisible side of it. This is the privilege of those who live on the edge of the purely human community: the infant, the old, the dead, and the ritualists, shamans or initiates of the medicine societies. They are able to meet with the most powerful, therefore the most visible, of the powers or spirits. What must be noted, however, is that the powers are always present, informing the daily reality, whether they are perceived or not.

In *Surfacing*, the heroine achieves a state of mind introducing her to a reality which has integrated at least part of the supernatural into the natural through the intermediacy of spirits conjured formally by rituals, and of ghosts — her parents, and infants — both her dead child and the newly conceived embryo. Yet to achieve a true vision, she has to relinquish the normal world and accept a transformation of her being, a literally altered state of consciousness through which the transfigured state of nature can be perceived. Instead of being, as in the Indian world, a revelation of a power or powers sustaining the daily reality and always lurking behind the ordinary, the vision is a once-in-a-lifetime occurrence triggered by and for the sake of the heroine herself. For her this new way of seeing is overlaid upon the memory of a faith shared by human people who used to live there and which was once used to gain the allegiance of the powers she now sees. This is the strongest element contributed to the novel by the Indian theme: without the Indian beliefs, the horned water god could not be present.

THE SHAMANIC TRADITION

The very concept of shamanism is elusive. According to certain authors, including Mircea Eliade,[7] we can talk about shamanism because it is possible to recognize similar patterns, symbols, rituals, and beliefs widely spread among many, if not all, cultures. However, from an ethnological point of view, it would be more proper to speak of shamans but not of shamanism, since no common doctrine has been identified so far.[8] In any case, the term *shamanism* in ethnographic parlance does not apply to all North American Indian cosmologies or rituals, nor can we use the term to designate the entire religious or philosophical system of any of these cultures. As a label, shamanism denotes a precise but varying set of beliefs, methods, and techniques aimed at the development of extraordinary mental, personal powers linked to the central notion of the existence of human and non-human souls and their independent survival when separated from the body which once supported them. This development takes place in a given cultural context usually based on hunting-gathering subsistence, though in a number of cultures we find shamanism side by side with rituals and beliefs which fall outside the shamanic realm. But some cultures are dominated by the shamanic rituals and the belief system which supports them (or did at one time since now, for the most part, such rituals and beliefs are no longer transmitted, no longer spoken of among the descendants of the peoples from whom Europeans learned about them).

Once established in a culture, shamanism is extremely pervasive and can be traced through many aspects of life. Hunting becomes a shamanic ritual as is every dealing with animals or plants and with certain natural events or forces which are all thought to be endowed with a soul. Birth, death, and especially episodes of sickness are seen and explained from a point of view in which the soul and its universe take precedence over physical causality.[9]

The techniques used by the shamans are known: a controlled trance state of varying intensity, including the dream state, allowing access to different perceptions of reality. These perceptions are controlled by "helpers" or "guardian spirits" who are beings or representations of beings, usually of an animal nature, who are encountered during the initiation phase and who become the assistants of the shaman and the focus of his or her power. The initiation is constructed around a death and rebirth scenario acted in the solitude of the initiate's own mind and the wilderness of the woods, mountains, or tundra. As all learning is thought to come from within the seeker's mind and soul, there is little explicit teaching. Fasting, purification rituals, bathing in cold water, exposure to cold, lack of sleep, and drugs may be used to induce the first visions or meetings, but the powers themselves decide who will be elected. Their first manifestation is usually in the form of a sickness which is overcome only when the novice shaman accepts the call and its consequences and retreats from the human community to experience the ordeal of violent symbolic death accompanied by a meeting with the powers, face-to-face. Whether slowly eaten, dismembered, drowned, or cooked by the spirits, the shaman is dehumanized, only the skeleton of his or her former self remaining. The shaman is then put back together and returns to the human world, having acquired the powers or gifts inherent in his or her experience of the non-human world.

In spite of its possible violence, the shamanic experience is described by its practitioners in terms of ecstasy, light, completion, and transfiguration. As the shamans' skills grow, they learn to control their powers, helpers, or gifts. They acquire one of the traditional hallmarks of shamanic experience: shamanic flight, in which they have the impression that they are separating from their bodies, floating away in either a flight or a dive. Once out of their bodies, they can travel over the country, explore the depths of the ocean, go to the land of the dead, examine their dream worlds, or see their reality, including their patients, in a different manner.

If the vision in which we participate in *Surfacing* appears coloured by Amerindian themes, the tale of the quest itself reflects even more strongly the vision quest of the traditional Algonkian Indian cultures. Among North American Indians, the concept of quest is associated most intimately with the concept of vision on one hand, and that of guardian spirit or helper on the other. But in the Algonkian traditions, the same complex informs both the life cycle of the laymen through the vision quest undertaken by the youths and the acquisition of powers by the shamans.

From this perspective, the central motif in the multi-dimensional search presented in *Surfacing* is the dialogue between the heroine and her "helpers." The other motifs, such as the search for the father or the resurrection of the child within her, appear then as necessary means by which such dialogue can be established. And dialogue is established in similar ways by Indian seekers and Atwood's narrator. In the case of Indian seekers, a retreat away from the human community leads to a patient wait for signs, visions, or dreams expressing the presence and guidance of the supernatural helpers. The usual hunger, thirst, sleep-deprivation and other painful disciplines accompanying the quest are aimed at provoking the pity of the spirits who are further placated by offerings and prayers. In addition, an attitude of humility is a prerequisite to any contact with the non-human world. Various modes of purification — such as bathing, fasting, and taking emetics — are also used, while taboos regarding daily life are more strictly enforced to prepare the seeker mentally as well as physically to meet with the powers and to be accepted by them. Dreams are seen either as channels through which the powers might express themselves or as steps preparatory to that expression.

In *Surfacing*, this dialogue demands a similar and very explicit retreat from humanity, expressed in a physical and mental separation, in a re-absorption of the seeker into the natural wilderness, and in a refusal of human speech. Throughout the novel, the attitude of the heroine toward language evolves. First comes the discovery that language may be meaningless:

> My throat constricts, as it learned to do when I discovered people could say words that would go into my ears meaning nothing. To be deaf and dumb would be easier. (*Sfg*, p. 11)

If language may be wrong, if words can lie, if laughter itself can be "canned" as another product of the "American" disease, then to speak the truth becomes a prerequisite for any search. When words fail to convey reality or cannot be understood anymore, silence is the only alternative. Language is both an obstacle to one's endeavour and a sign of one's humanity that must be left behind with the rest.

It is significant that all contacts with the powers and "spirits" are conveyed through images and feeling, never through words. When the heroine visualizes the birth of her new child, she specifies that she "will never teach it any words" (*Sfg*, p. 162). Yet the return to the human world when all is done implies a recognition of language. The child itself will have to learn for there are "Word furrows potential already in its proto-brain, untravelled paths" (*Sfg*, p. 191). The last page of the novel contains the final admission that "For us it's necessary, the intercession of words" (*Sfg*, p. 192). Although this view of the necessity of language contrasts finally with the Indian view, which extends the human gift of language to all powerful beings whether human or not, it does nevertheless express a will to get closer to, or even merge with nature, the silent trees, the quiet lake, things originally without names.

This transformation into, or return to, an animal state — that of the wild woman — also calls to mind the power attributed to Algonkian shamans to change themselves into animals, as well as the Northwestern Canadian Indian belief that uncontrolled contact with wild powers, whether animal or mythic, may remove the seeker from the human world or sever his connections with the human community. Hence it is necessary to "tame" the initiate back into his human nature. But such transformations are seen much more as a consequence of power attained but not controlled, sometimes as a gift, often as an accident. In *Surfacing*, however, the transformation seems to be more of a means of allowing the heroine to continue her quest or even a necessary step in its achievement.

Through ritual gestures allowing both distance and contact Atwood's heroine defines and understands the new reality. Perhaps because of the definitions of the powers involved, the ritual gestures connected with them are much closer to the Algonkian ceremonials, especially when dealing with the horned water god and the human ghosts. Yet very few of these gestures are explicitly presented as rituals in the text. Two of them are offerings and are taken from the Indian cosmology as learned by the heroine. First she acknowledges her debt to the gods behind the petroglyphs by leaving a piece of her clothing as an offering (*Sfg*, p. 145). This gesture corresponds directly to a widespread Amerindian custom of making offerings to the powers inhabiting the cliffs stamped with rock paintings. Tobacco, clothing, bundles of coloured sticks, and food were left there, especially in Ojibwa territory.

Later, a seemingly innocuous offering marks another stage of the heroine's quest, the summons to her parents' ghosts:

> I cleared the table and scraped the canned ham fat scraps from the plates into the fire, food for the dead. If you fed them enough they would come back; or was it the reverse, if you fed them enough they would stay away, it was in one of the books but I'd forgotten. (*Sfg*, p. 155)

A continent-wide custom for the Amerindian people, this offering to the dead is connected to their view of fire as the most direct link with or passage toward the dead and toward the animal. Like ritual offerings, this summons is part of a ceremonial context whereby contact was maintained with the non-human world which used to be a matter of daily concern for the Algonkian people — it was not restricted to the occasion of the vision quest itself.

A closer look at the text reveals other gestures which are associated with purification, including bathing and fasting, taboos, prayers, and visions. The concept of retreat from the human community is emphasized by the choice of an island as the main locus of the story. The concept of fasting can be followed easily enough in the heroine's attempt to avoid human food. To recognize Amerindian practices in these acts, the Algonkian customs may be set against these elements of *Surfacing*, but the similarities which then appear are immediately counterbalanced by the obvious differences. While the Algonkian initiate is looking for a life-long acquaintance with the powers sustaining his life, the heroine of *Surfacing* is going through a period of apparent insanity. The distance between the two points of view is further reflected in the ways in which dreams are handled in each of them. For the Algonkian, as for seekers in all North American Indian cultures, dreams are the ideal medium for a meeting with the power world. Dreams, once controlled, are the main tool of the shamans and other healers, and are most often considered to be one type of vision. A shaman's initiatory dream always involves a transformation of the person. It is a transformation which is at once inescapable, profound, and definitive (unless stopped and counteracted by extraordinary means). Such a contact announces the emergence of a more-than-human or paranormal or spiritual component in the person, and it signals the sometimes violent, sometimes progressive metamorphosis of the shaman as the new power or powers inform and shape their host. Thus the acquisition of power, indicated among other things by the ability to see what is hidden to others, is intimately linked to an inner transformation of the person: the shaman is not totally human anymore — human, that is, in terms of the culture in which the shaman was born. The shamanic adventure is a plunge into temporary and controlled insanity, followed by a transformation of personality, of one's universe, and a change which is so profound that it is almost always expressed by initiates in physiological as well as psychological terms. During rituals the shaman will go back toward this new world, this other state of being which is also ecstacy.

What happens in *Surfacing* is very different from this. The heroine comes back from her dive into wilderness to re-possess herself, her memory, her normalcy. She has gained acceptance of herself and reality. She is now fully herself and fully human. The only common point here between the two would be that both the shaman and the heroine are seeking completeness, but the shaman's is of a different order. The heroine finds in the wilderness the strength and the roots which allow her to regain her humanity; the shaman seeks contact with the non-human part of himself. The narrator's description of her goals follows definite stages: a reunion of two severed halves, a bringing together of head (thought and reason) and body (physical reactions and emotions), a healing. She knows that she cannot live as a wild woman and that wilderness is not her final goal. Having concluded the vision cycles, she is drawn back to the cabin, to civilization, to culture. The shaman, on the other hand, stays in the wood, tracking and goading the elusive powers of the wilderness of nature and mind, and going fully through the very insanity which the heroine cannot afford because she must return to a world in which these powers are ignored at best and often regarded as a sign of madness or worse. She is also constrained by the fact that she comes from that world. She cannot manage the shaman's skills and methods which allow the initiate to control the powers that were met and set in motion, to bring their gifts back and to reintegrate into the human community, often to the benefit of that community. She would have no protection, no support, no teacher or training, no ritual, no myth, no map to help her find her way.

In *Surfacing*, therefore, the essence of the shamanic world is absent; the initiation does not lead to the emergence of an initiate but to a return to normal humanity, a return following a deep crisis, but nevertheless a return which does not fulfil the promises offered by the same rituals in the shamanic context. The scale of the means used by the heroine to reconquer her lost memory and her soul gives a monumental aspect to the crisis through which she has passed. She has been healed and made whole and now carries a life, or a potential for life, in her womb. She has experienced the continuity of life, the symbolic merging of all happenings in a common scenario, the unity of all perception. This, at least, may remain with her, but what language, what ritual, will she be able to use to express this new perception? She must translate the knowledge she has gained into concern for the normal side of herself, of her dead parents, and of the world around her. She can no longer extend herself to the mystical, the spiritual.

What is missing in the world of *Surfacing* is the elusive quality without which no statement can be totally meaningful, no cultural environment totally satisfying: a general coherence, a sense of connection between the different parts and levels. Culture, ultimately, is not the content or even the structure of our human environment, but what binds the content and keeps the structure together. We can apply to the shaman in a direct way what is valid for all members of a given culture, the more so as the shaman operates explicitly to transcend the known world of his community in order to go toward an often undefined unknown. In one of the most powerful statements for the understanding of the shamanic enterprise and its relationship to the culture which supports it, Edward Sapir writes:

> Once the individual self has grown strong enough to travel in the path most clearly illuminated by its own light, it not only can but should discard much of the scaffolding by which it has made its ascent . . . If the traveling in the path of the self's illumination leads to a position that is destructive of the very values the self was fed on . . . it has not in the slightest lost touch with genuine culture. It may well, on the contrary, have arrived at its own highest possible point of culture development.[10]

A shaman is an individual who at least temporarily forsakes his cultural background to launch himself toward the unknown, toward regions that are ill-defined or, at the limit, not defined by the cosmology shared by the community. The paradox is, of course, that the shaman could not succeed in his enterprise were his cultural environment too weak or were he not thoroughly grounded in it.

In *Surfacing*, however, we have a vision of our own fragmented culture in which the few moments of coherence are marked or introduced by signs recalling the unbroken world of the previous inhabitants of this land. The environment of Atwood's heroine appears to be almost a non-culture, for the coherence which may seem to be the most important quality of the North American Indian cultures is not transmitted along with the objects and symbols taken out of their original cultural context. The narrator's return to a silent community is evidence of the failure of our civilization to provide a meaningful context to her life. However, I am not sure that this implicit condemnation of our society does justice to the realities of most contemporary lives. The "Americans" of the book are the living dead not because they kill, not because they kill with machines, but because they kill without meaning. Is meaning to be provided by society or by culture alone, or should we, like the shamans of old, seek for it beyond a known but no longer sufficient world? This is the problem finally faced by *Surfacing*.

Notes

1. Selwyn Dewdney, *Dating Rock Art in the Canadian Shield Region* (Toronto: Royal Ontario Museum Occasional Paper 24, 1970), p. 5.
2. Selwyn Dewdney and Kenneth E. Kidd, *Indian Rock Paintings of the Great Lakes*, 2nd ed. (Toronto: University of Toronto Press, 1967), pp. 168-69.

3. Campbell Grant, *Rock Art of the American Indian* (New York: Crowell, 1967), p. 147.
 4. Dewdney and Kidd, *Indian Rock Paintings*, p. 172.
 5. A. Irving Hallowell, *Culture and Experience* (Philadelphia: University of Pennsylvania Press, 1955), p. 104.
 6. A. Irving Hallowell, *Contributions to Anthropology* (Chicago and London: University of Chicago Press, 1976), pp. 405, 415–16.
 7. Mircea Eliade, *Shamanism: Archaic Techniques of Ecstasy*, trans. Willard R. Trask (New York: Pantheon Books, 1964).
 8. See R. Boyer and E. Lot-Falck, ed., *Les réligions de l'Europe du Nord* (Paris: Fayard-Denoel, 1974).
 9. See Marie-Françoise Guédon, "Chamanisme Athapaskan," in *Proceedings of the Canadian Ethnology Society Conference* (Ottawa: National Museum of Man, 1974), pp. 82-85.
10. Edward Sapir, "Culture, Genuine and Spurious" (1924), repr. in David G. Mandelbaum, ed., *Selected Writings of Edward Sapir in Language, Culture and Personality* (Berkeley and Los Angeles: University of California Press, 1949), p. 324.

7

The Uses Of Ambiguity:
Margaret Atwood and Hubert Aquin

Philip Stratford

Hubert Aquin's novels are fugitive, elusive, marked by an ambiguity that is due in part to his conception of the art form, in part to the historical situation in which his fiction is rooted. His is a universe of mirrors and double images in which all symmetrical elements tend to a point of convergence which, in turn, is constantly vanishing. Aquin is a double agent tracking down an elusive enemy brother who is none other than his own image in the mirror but which at the same time is also an image of Quebec and of modern man. His work embodies a search for equilibrium in a world that is profoundly divided and where man lives forever divorced from himself and from others. It takes up the central theme of Quebec fiction — alienation, with its familiar components of obsession with the absolute, flight, and the sense of vertigo — but with the conscious intent of putting an end to this alienation and of taking possession of life in all its relativity, fragmentation and discontinuity.[1]

Patricia Smart's introductory description of Hubert Aquin's fiction could be applied with little alteration to Margaret Atwood's. Her novels contain the same cultivated ambiguity, stemming from what she has called the "paranoid schizo-phrenia" (*JSM*, p. 62) of the Canadian psyche. It surfaces in her own work in images of mirrors that reflect frightening yet fraternal images of the self. A rankling sense of alienation permeates all her fiction, expressed in the neurotic edginess of her prose and in images of death and drowning, yet not leading to total despair but to the desire for a more inclusive life reconciling hitherto unmanage-able complexities.

It is tempting to take a lead like this and by careful cross-reading to multiply the evidences of similarity. In fact it is a necessary first step in comparison. But beyond the likenesses are nuances of difference, not individual but collective, not thematic but stylistic, which lead much farther into an understanding of particular works of these two novelists and their distinctive cultural contexts.

Surfacing and *Prochain Episode*, their titles echoing the qualified hope that ends each novel, are the two representative works I wish to examine. Aquin's first novel, published in 1965 when he was thirty-six, startled the critics by its brilliance. As an editor of *Liberté* (1961), essayist for *parti pris* and author of scenarios for the NFB and of TV dramas for Radio-Canada, Aquin was not unknown, but his work was dispersed and lacked the focus he was to give it in this and his three subsequent novels. *Prochain Episode*, opening a remarkable publishing season in Quebec which also saw Marie-Claire Blais' *Une saison dans la vie d'Emmanuel* and Réjean Ducharme's *L'Avalée des avalées*, established Aquin as one of the foremost writers of his generation.

In the same way, several years later, Margaret Atwood's *Surfacing* (1972) confirmed her as a major novelist. Although ten years younger than Aquin, she had already established a solid reputation as a poet by the time of her first novel, *The Edible Woman* (1969). She continued to publish important poetry. This and her controversial critical overview of Canadian literature, *Survival* (1972), which was also a justification of her own creative views and a programme for her fiction, paved the way for *Surfacing*.

Just as rapprochements can be made between the place of these novels in their authors' careers, so certain biographical details situate the writers on the same comparative wave-length. Both grew up in the bourgeois mainstream. Atwood studied English at Toronto followed by postgraduate work at Radcliffe: Aquin, history at l'Université de Montréal followed by studies at The Faculté des Sciences Politiques in Paris. After some experience of the business world, both did a spell of university teaching, although it is appropriate to note here that it is more customary for Quebec writers to support themselves by journalism than to work the university circuit. Atwood's connection with the Toronto publishing house Anansi corresponds to Aquin's affiliation with Montreal's *Liberté* and *parti pris*, connections which situate them in the vanguard of the literary intelligentsia of the 1960's. Both were outspoken nationalists, though of course the lines they took on colonialism and imperialism have different co-ordinates. Yet while they are committed writers they are not factious, and both have been sharply critical of their own literary and political milieu, Atwood's description of the victim syndrome in Canadian literature finding its counterpart in Aquin's diagnosis of "La fatigue culturelle du Canada français."[2] Frank Davey sets Atwood's dominance of English-Canadian letters from 1966 to 1973 which corresponds exactly to the period of Aquin's greatest influence in Quebec.

But these resemblances are accessories before the fact, and the facts I wish to examine are the novels themselves. We may begin with Aquin and a general description: the popular model for *Prochain Episode* is the thriller. It is a story of espionage and counter-espionage complete with international intrigue in Lausanne, Geneva, and Montreal; detection, pursuit, capture, and escape; aliases, codes, a web of contradictory clues and deceiving discoveries, in short, it uses all the paraphernalia and clichés of the genre.

The unnamed narrator's mission is assassination. He must track down and kill one H. de Heutz in collaboration with his blonde fellow-agent and lover, K. But who is de Heutz? At the critical moment he uses the narrator's own cover story and their identities meld. And is K an ally or a counter-revolutionary agent? Unnerved by these confusions, the narrator fails in his Swiss mission, and on his return to Montreal he is picked up and incarcerated. He writes the story of his frustrations and perplexities from cell CG 19 in a psychiatric hospital where he is being held for examination.

The spy story itself is, however, only a vehicle for the true intrigue, and the real interest of the novel lies in the complex picture the narrator gives of himself while drawing the reader on in the story of his adventures. Espionage is a metaphor for the identification, pursuit, and attempted capture of the elusive self.

It is harder to assign a conventional and popular model to *Surfacing*, unless it is the juvenile mystery story. It too is a novel of discovery. It uses a search motif as frame; in this case another nameless first-person narrator seeks to unravel a mystery, that of her father's disappearance from an island in a lake in Northern Quebec. With three city friends, one of them her lover, she returns to this childhood home and, after exploring the territory in widening circles, pieces together clues her father has left behind and finally discovers his drowned body. But the description of the search is simply narrative bait. What the heroine is really exploring and discovering is herself. In place of the sophisticated European references which give density and glamour to Aquin's story, Atwood's novel introduces the exotica of the Canadian wilderness, its flora and fauna, and the mores of living in the bush. The two novels make an interesting complementary pair, representing as they do polarities in Canadian cultural experience: on the one hand, confrontation with the heavy heritage of the Old World, on the other, confrontation with the hostile environment of the New. Alienation in time, one might say, oversimplifying, vis-à-vis alienation in space.

But before examining further the central themes of the books, let us first look at the way they are expressed by comparing opening chapters. Despite the common theme of search, the procedures of discovery are radically different. Aquin's hero is chronically voluble and articulate. Though full of self-doubt, he is remorselessly self-aware. From the very first page he bares himself to the reader in a glut of turbulent confession. His self-consciousness extends immediately to speculation about the kind of book he is writing (the one being read). First, he toys with the idea of setting it in "the mainstream of the spy-story tradition,"[3] then he tries an invented hero, but after half a page he abandons this strategy for introspection. Fragments of memories surface and then are swept away in gloomy meditation on his present state. The narrative develops in a series of backward loops with a wide range of historical and literary allusion. This soliloquy, a form of direct revelation yet obscured by the extreme fluidity of the hero's outpourings, continues for the first three chapters. It is not until Chapter 4, one-fifth of the way through the book, that a more conventional type of narration begins with the narrator now established as hero of his own spy story, and even so, the rehearsal of events is frequently interrupted by long stretches of Hamlet-like reflection.

Atwood's novel is also confessional, but in another convention. Its progression is firmly linear; from the first sentence it moves forward in clearly identifiable space. Different things observed on the road home spark sharp memories of the heroine's past, and interference is set up between "then" and "now." But the narrative line remains straight and clear, the convention requiring that the reader live experience at the same pace as it unfolds to the narrator. The question of the narrative as a possible artifice is never raised.

The narrator herself, however, is far from straight or clear. Before long the reader realizes that she is dramatically conceived and hides or falsifies as much as she reveals. Her limited credibility is accepted, but her cutting, skewed observations, the inconsistencies in what she recalls of her past, and even her choppy syntax betray the fact that she is deeply disturbed. As the novel progresses, she grows painfully in self-knowledge and the reader's discovery of concealed areas of her life and character matches her own. The important point to emphasize is that the novel moves forward towards a more and more complete revelation. An expectation of progress through experience and analysis of experience animates the heroine's search for her father and herself.

In contrast, Aquin's hero's mission is as reflexive, circular, and inconclusive as the manner of its telling. The superficial activity of the spy story thinly disguises the fact that this is not history, not even a case history, but the unveiling of a particular state of mind. Any idea of progress or finality in the search for self is precluded. The hero delivers himself entire from the very first; revelation, instead of being progressive, is rather the multiple illumination of a complex static state.

Having established these basic differences in the manner of narration we can return to theme to compare the source and nature of the narrators' alienations, for a common characteristic is that both are profoundly alienated. From the start, Atwood's heroine unconsciously reveals that she suffers from a deep-seated dualism. Not only do the "then" and "now" of past memories and present experience enter into conflict, but she also nervously registers many dichotomies between city and wilderness and is hypersensitive to much supposed hostility between "me" and "them." The threatening "them" has many variants. In one sense "they" are her city friends, clichés of the consumer society of the 1960's: male-chauvinist David with his knee-jerk reactions and his ever-ready camera levelled like a gun at random samples of country kitsch, Anna his slave-wife with her banal songs, her make-up mask, and the imprisoning mirror of her compact, and inarticulate, animal-like Joe, the narrator's lover. Although they are her best friends (she has known Anna two months), seen against the background of her old home, her otherness is accentuated. However, she is no closer to the Québécois villagers, her parents' local contacts. For that matter, she has also become estranged from her parents; they too have become "they." Later, and very pervasively, "they" becomes Americans, "Bloody fascist pig Yanks" (*Sfg*, p. 9) in David's automatic phrase, or anyone associated with American values. And in the background of her consciousness, firmly repressed, lurks a mysterious "He," her ex-husband (?) and father of her dead child (?).

Added to these evidences of alienation are many signs of moral disgust and confusion. Images of dismemberment abound. The artificiality of a commercialized urban environment has tainted the North and its phoniness has infected her friends. The heroine is disoriented, calls "home ground" "foreign territory" (*Sfg*, p. 11), does not know the way, feels she is in "the wrong place" (*Sfg*, p. 8), states: "I feel deprived of something, as though I can't really get here unless I've suffered" (*Sfg*, p. 15). But she is unable to feel, let alone suffer. Confronted by her alienation, fear, and guilt, she experiences the temptation to filter out pain and embarrassment: "To be deaf and dumb would be easier" (*Sfg*, p. 11). From memories of vomiting to thoughts of violent highway death, the first chapter is full of references that point up a state of emotional repulsion and instability barely under control.

At least Aquin's hero does not suffer from repression. His response to alienation is not frigidity but volatility. His confinement is physical; he liberates himself through the direct expression of his fears and frustrations. The general characteristics of his alienation, however, duplicate those of Atwood's heroine. He too acutely experiences internal divisions, a sense of solitude and of his own otherness, moral disgust, disorientation, and the wish to escape pain by anaesthesia. But there is no need to decode the expression of his *malaise*. He states his own symptoms directly, perhaps overstates them, for compared to those of Atwood's heroine they are always more extreme. Where she feels discomfort, he faces despair; where she remembers nausea, he wrestles with vertigo; her sense of disorientation in space is his in time: "I am losing track . . . even of time itself, for I have no fixed point from which to measure" (*PE*, p. 12); her feeling of exclusion is the fact of his imprisonment; her wish for numbness is his fear of madness; he takes her self-doubt as far as thoughts of suicide; her nervous tension takes on manic-depressive proportions in his case as he veers rapidly between elation and despair.

An interesting comparative question is raised here. Does the reader, noting these differences in intensity, but also noting underlying similarities in the general diagnosis of a common alienation, stress what is common in theme and conclude that the two novels are quite like, or emphasize the differences in style and insist on their dissimilarity? The answer is, of course, that both observations must be given due weight; even if contradictory, they co-exist and illuminate one another. Any discriminating comparison must comprehend both poles.

To examine the pole of difference then, the relative importance given to indirect or direct expression by Atwood and Aquin might be said to resemble the two terms of a metaphor. To take an example, the heroine of *Surfacing* thinks of her parents as "going about their own concerns closed safe behind a wall as translucent as jello, mammoths frozen in a glacier" (*Sfg*, p. 9). While respecting both terms of the proposition "parents are mammoths" — the one, "parents," general and straightforward, the other, "mammoths" specific but oblique — one may react more strongly to the first term or to the second. One may retain the idiosyncrasy of "mammoths" and move on metonymically from there, or one may find "mammoths" more important for the way it throws light back on "parents" and, consequently, let the significance of "parents" dominate the sharpness of the second term. French usage, at least to the English reader, seems to favour the latter emphasis, the weight falling on the first, more abstract and general term of the metaphor. The use of metaphor in English, on the other hand, tends to count more on the specificity of Eliot's objective correlative and to accentuate the second term of the metaphor. The difference can be apprehended by comparing one of Aquin's metaphors to the one just given from Atwood. "This disorderly creation is my bulwark against the violent waves of sadness and guilt, pounding out the name of the woman I love" (*PE*, p. 11). In this metaphor, although it is a complex one, the disorder, sadness and guilt, that is, the general terms, take precedence over the more concrete elements, "bulwark," "waves," and "pounding."

Space does not permit a further examination of this theoretical detour. But that the point does have a practical incidence will be apparent to anyone who has tried to translate French verse. The problem for the English translator is always how to make his way among what might loosely be called "so many abstractions." Conversely, this explains why French readers of English verse so often find it anecdotal, materialistic, pedestrian, in the extreme, trivial.

With regard to *Surfacing* and *Prochain Episode*, there is not only a difference of intensity in narration but also a difference, thinking of these remarks on metaphor, in directness and specificity of statement. As has been observed, Atwood's narration is closed, Aquin's open. It is also dramatic compared to his lyrical, or, to choose a period distinction, Metaphysical to his Romantic. And Atwood's narrative is full of details, objective correlatives whose emotional springs the reader must imaginatively deduce. Aquin's novel, on the contrary, provides, in the most direct way, a plethora of open, lyrical, romantic, direct statements about the narrator's plight.

Of course these differences are not just particular to Atwood and Aquin. These characteristics can be differentiated, linguistically, even imaginatively, as French and English, and on the local level can be seen as collective attributes of Quebec and English-Canadian novels. The general stylistic differences between other pairs of Canadian novelists — Roy and MacLennan, for instance, Langevin and Ross, Hébert and Laurence, Blais and Munro, or Carrier and Kroetsch — demonstrate the collective common denominator.

But here it might be argued that although in some respects Atwood and Aquin may conform to their "national" types, in other respects they are atypical. The international scope of Aquin's fiction, for example, sets it aside from most contemporary Quebec fiction; his use of the European model of the spy story makes him unique. Despite what has just been said about his use, compared to Atwood, of a general and abstract vocabulary of self-analysis, it is also true that, compared to other Quebec novelists, he is lavish in his use of detail, so much so that, as Ronald Sutherland notes[4], parts of *Prochain Episode* read like a Baedeker to the Swiss Alps or remind other critics of the object-cluttered fiction of the French *Nouvelle Vague*.

By the same token, although Margaret Atwood writes in the main English-Canadian tradition where documentary realism is the fictional staple, she also moves outside the expected norms. In *Surfacing* observed fact blends with personal fantasy, detail is used not only as document but also as poetry, and her novel, although it has the lineaments of a case history, also symbolically portrays a state of mind, an *état d'âme*, very much in the style of Quebec fiction.

These apparently uncharacteristic features warrant closer investigation. In the chase part of *Prochain Episode* (chapters 5 to 17, less three chapters of self-analysis), detail abounds. There is a glossy catalogue of names of streets, towns, peaks, cars, cafés, foods, wines, *objets d'art*. The text is punctuated with specific times, dates, prices, licence-plate numbers, and acronyms. What is the purpose of such precise inside information? Does it serve, as Sutherland suggests, to "keep the book from becoming overcharged with emotion"?[5] Undoubtedly, linked to the pursuit theme, such details do provide a fast change of pace from the narrator's turgid, self-scrutinizing ramblings. They seduce the reader by their Fleming-like connoisseurship. They give a hard edge to the narrative. To that extent Sutherland is right.

On the other hand, detail as Aquin uses it has relatively little documentary significance; it has nothing to do with social realism or *réalité sociale*. The repetition of proper nouns acts poetically, like incantation. Details belong to the abracadabra of the pursuit-fiction genre; though meticulously accurate, they are insignificant in themselves, as neutral as information in a guidebook. This is not detail lovingly accumulated for accuracy of statement or precision of recall or used as an objective correlative for emotion. No, beneath the surface glitter, such details are unsubstantial, artificial, abstract. They do, of course, serve a purpose. They provide a context for the chase which itself, with its accelerations and decompressions, its doublings back, its confusion of identities and its sudden alternations between euphoria and discouragement, frenetic action and helpless stasis, is a metaphor for the narrator's tumultuous state of mind. Here is the reality of the fiction, and it is strictly a psychological reality. The detail helps describe the landscape of the mind rather than some external landscape.

One example is the detailed inventory of the furnishings of H. de Heutz's château at Echandens in chapter 13, (pp. 90-102). This is a symbolic recital rather than an informative or necessary adjunct to the development of the action. The Louis XIII buffet with its carved door depicting a naked warrior is referred to five times in twelve pages; the lacquered commode decorated with a combat between two soldiers, three times (and twice in the next chapter); Stoffel's *History of Julius Caesar*, twice; Benjamin West's engraving of "The Death of General Wolfe," five times. Of course all these *objets d'art* have allusive significance hinted at by the hero: the naked warrior is himself, the two soldiers, himself and de Heutz, there is a link between Stoffel's book and the lecture de Heutz ostensibly gave on Caesar's battle with the "courageous Helvetians" who are likened to the Québécois revolutionaries, and another between Wolfe and de Heutz, agent of the Crown soon to be brought down in another battle for Quebec. The collection as a whole fills the narrator with admiration, stressing his aesthete's inertia and his confused sense of identity with his intended victim.

But even more important to note is the way the significance of these objects changes while the narrator waits, gun in hand, for the arrival of de Heutz. As his purpose cools, the "splendid museum" (*PE*, p. 99) becomes "a decorated cage" (*PE*, p. 100), becomes "this gallery of oneiric emblems" (*PE*, p. 100). "My destiny," the narrator reflects, "clothed in damask linen and imaginary furniture, closes in on me, pitilessly" (*PE*, p. 100). The room "seems to freeze me in eternity, a naked and helpless warrior" (*PE*, p. 101). The objects, then, are less important in themselves than as mirrors of the hero's mind, and detail is part of the narrator's kaleidoscopic recital, not so much of real events as of the activity of his psyche. Detail is used to persuade the reader of the reality of a day-dream or nightmare rather than to give a convincing picture of a real world.

Seeking an analogue one might compare the narrative use Atwood makes of her heroine's father's sketches of the rock painting. They are important objects in their own right; they are vitally and directly connected to the plot; they have meaning and demand interpretation. Once the puzzle of their literal meaning is solved, they take on deeper meaning for the heroine as guidelines, as a posthumous "gift" (*Sfg*, p. 146) from her father, forcing the narrator and reader once again to search for their significance; they stand for something outside the heroine to be acquired by her; they are never only mirror-like projections of her own mental processes.

With respect to Aquin's use of detail it is interesting to look at other themes in the novel, although the quantity is considerably less. The love theme is one example — the narrator's relationship with K. It is much less precisely described than his pursuit of H. de Heutz; still, in the same way, it partakes of manic-depressive ups and downs, moments of total elation and complete dejection, and tells more about the hero's mind than it does about an actual love affair. On a thematic level, the de Heutz mission represents the failure of the revolution while the vague but passionate K episodes represent its inspiration. But the revolutionary programme itself is never precisely described. It remains the implied motive force of the plot but also remains cryptic. The revolutionary plan and its failure is less important in fact than it is as an image of the narrator's troubled psyche as he veers from the urge for freedom and fulfilment to frustration and dejected imprisonment. In the same way, the act of writing the novel, the driving impulse to create something original, the disordered result, and the narrator's meditations on his own impotence give yet another image of his mental turmoil.

Creative, sexual, revolutionary, or political drives and their frustration are constantly intermingled and are all facets of a single reality: the narrator's. To subordinate this reality to any one of these themes (it is most tempting to choose the revolutionary) is to miss the main focus of the novel which is not, after all, an action-packed, detail-crammed spy story but a close examination of the erratic workings of the hero's state of mind and possibly of a collective one, very close to the central tradition of Québec fiction.

Further consideration of Margaret Atwood's use of detail in *Surfacing* will accentuate and clarify the difference. Atwood's novel is more case history than psychic projection. Though obsessed by history, Aquin's hero, like his country, has "no history" (*PE*, p. 70). No physical description of him is ever given, no *curriculum vitae*; he has no family, no childhood, no career, no existence outside his terrorist activity. His friends, if they are his friends, all go by aliases. He himself is nameless, pastless, faceless. The reader knows everything that goes on in his mind but practically nothing about him. As in many Québec novels, the hero is a floating consciousness which readers are free to flesh out by furnishing their own or, more likely, collective attributes and characteristics.

Atwood's heroine is nameless too, but she has a heavy, though buried, individual past. In fact, in her present state of numbness the past is all she seems to have: "To have the past but not the present, that means you're going senile" (*Sfg*, p. 73). A good part of the book is spent identifying the past and assimilating it to the present as she returns, literally and symbolically, to try to find her father. Some of this recapture has the documentary astringency of, say, Alice Munro or Margaret Laurence; for example, in the passages where she recalls Sunday-school or childhood birthday parties. In such passages the narrator is concerned to get the factual, social, and emotional shading exactly right. The event recalled has its own objective importance even without being related to the character of the narrator and her drama. (One could hardly say the same of the detailed information provided by Aquin's narrator.)

More difficult for the heroine is the recall of her recent past, fogged and blocked as it is by the trauma of her unhappy love affair in the city and her abortion. Here detail is fragmented and coloured by her present guilt and alienation. It is half-imagined, half-recalled, the proportion of accurate recall increasing as the heroine becomes more and more master of her situation. The analogue for this is the K affair in *Prochain Episode*, though even when she is fantasizing about a repressed experience, Atwood's heroine uses much more concrete detail than Aquin's hero.

At the level of present action, detail again has intrinsic importance. Through description of the subwilderness and the wilder island, the reader learns about a real environment (much more real at any rate than Aquin's Baedeker Switzerland). The domestic drama played out between David and Anna and David's and Joe's advances to the heroine, reveal not only the heroine's character but also the values of a generation of urban misfits who exist outside the heroine. (Neither de Heutz nor K has any self-substantial reality.)

The last part and climax of *Surfacing*, where the heroine, alone on the island, gives way to her madness and acts out her alienation by rebelling against her friends and stripping herself of all signs of civilization, is closest in narrative internalization to Aquin's fiction. Like the narrator in *Prochain Episode*, Atwood's heroine now lives with nightmarish intensity. Tracked like an animal in once-familiar surroundings, she reverts to an instinctive state, bows to primitive fears and taboos, sees visions, feels herself in the power of spirits, participates in the power, loses and regains it. But once again, although the narrative here is extraordinarily free and fluid and is mixed with high speculation, fantasy, and poetic statement, it is still filled with concrete detail. Also, although this is the most direct expression of the heroine's state of mind in the book, it is important to note that the state is a transitory one, not constant as in Aquin's narrative. It is a stage through which the heroine passes. In the end she re-enters her own time; she refuses to be a victim; she sees herself in the glass as a natural woman; she is able to laugh; she accepts the child she is carrying; she rediscovers trust; she is ready to begin again. Joe returns to the island and calls her name.

Compared to the ending of *Prochain Episode* with its burst of violent revolutionary rhetoric, which is none the less simply the reiteration of frustration and anger that runs throughout the book, Atwood's conclusion is clearly of the progressive kind. The heroine has followed a certain linear narrative logic even if it is only, as she says at one time, the logic of her own madness. She has moved from passivity to action, has been brought face to face with her past, her suppressed problems, her self, and now stands on the threshold of something new. What it will be remains uncertain, but at least hitherto unformulated questions have now been asked. Progress has been made.

Atwood's narrator is dramatically conceived, as opposed to Aquin's more "lyrical" narrator. The time has come to look more closely at the dramatic nature of both novels. Atwood's is dramatic in that the heroine acts a drama by moving from a state of confusion to a state of resolution. The reader is intimately associated with her as she moves along this trajectory, but at the end she, like the reader, stands, as it were, outside her own drama looking back. Aquin's narrator, on the other hand, is never allowed this perspective, nor is his reader. First and last he is deeply and closely involved in his own drama, so caught up in it that he enjoys no distancing. If the figurative tense of Atwood's story is the past, that of Aquin's novel is the present, and the reader remains enclosed with him in the tumult of a present predicament. Dramatically speaking, we are not spectators but actors intensely involved to the point of being imprisoned with the narrator inside the action. In this way the narrative participates in the atmosphere of dream or nightmare mentioned above. One might compare Atwood's and Aquin's fictions as objective drama and subjective drama. Compared to Aquin's drama of dilemma, Atwood's seems purposeful, progressive and, yes, didactic.

This can be pointed up by looking at the political content of *Surfacing*. Most readers have been struck by the novel's strong anti-American slant. From the very first pages, the American presence in the Canadian wilderness is a target for the narrator's most cutting observations. The theme develops to embrace a whole mentality, passing through Malmstrom who wants to buy the island to the powerboat fishermen and heron-killers, and spreading eventually to include her friends David and Anna, creatures (as she is herself) of the superficial, sterile, mechanical, destructive aspects of modern life. Despite the fact that some ambiguity is allowed to play about the anti-American theme (the fishermen turn out to be Canadians, and the heroine's rejection of Americanism is part of her rejection of nearly everything else), it is strongly and consistently developed throughout the novel until it becomes a major focus for the heroine's anxiety and gives direction to her burst of climactic rebellious action and final self-discovery.

Atwood drives home her nationalistic theme in didactic fashion. One might have expected Aquin in the story of a Québec terrorist to identify the enemy clearly. But in *Prochain Episode* he is never really visible. In addition to the ambiguity that plays about the person of de Heutz and his various aliases, practically no explicit reference is made to the oppressive force against which the narrator is so passionately engaged. The revolutionary fever rages, but more or less in a void. All the features that have been singled out as differentiating these two fictions become operative again with regard to this subject. The hero's hatred and alienation in *Prochain Episode* has no clear objective correlative; the lack of objective detail is significant since it creates a vacuum which draws the reader in, requiring him to provide co-ordinates of interpretation from his own or from collective experience. The sharing of this unnamed but assumed anxiety makes the reader participate in a nightmarish perplexity; he is not so much an observer vicariously living out a specific action as an accomplice sharing the vagaries of a complex state of mind. The intent of the fiction is not to persuade the reader in didactic, albeit surprising, fashion of the inevitability of a certain line of argument, as much as to convince him of the inescapable necessity of assuming a certain attitude. It is not possible for him to draw conclusions; all he can do is submit fatalistically to vague but crippling constraints. He, like the narrator, is forced to see his predicament not in terms of an action developing sequentially from past to present but in terms of a continuous present. The fact of his imprisonment is a permanent psychological disability, not a temporal twist of plot. The drama of his situation is his being in it, not in the potentiality of his getting out of it. It is a drama of mental process, not one of moral progress.

On close examination, then, features of Aquin's and Atwood's fiction that at first seemed uncharacteristic of their respective cultural norms do in fact revert to type. And comparing the two novels shows that, despite many striking thematic similarities, they embody very different ideas about what a work of fiction should be and do.

Returning to the notion of ambiguity taken as a common point to open this essay, it is now evident that two different sorts are at work. Aquin's ambiguity draws the reader into a vortex of uncertainty and irresolution; Atwood's, applied dramatically to her narrator, leads into the novel but is progressively dissipated as the heroine moves towards a solution to her problems. Aquin's dualism is static, inescapable: two warriors locked in carved combat. Atwood's dualism is dynamic: her recognition of the head-body syndrome forces the heroine out of her inertia and frigidity. Both narrators are deeply alienated, but the nature of their alienation differs: Aquin's hero's frantic surface activity and the profusion of empty detail in which he indulges belie a chronic underlying sense of vertigo and imprisonment; Atwood's heroine makes a dizzying dive into her past, but she does surface again, freed of some of her illusions. She reaches the present. The future may be uncertain, but she is ready for a new start. At the end of *Prochain Episode* Aquin's hero says he is "sure of the future" and proclaims a revolutionary new beginning. But the novel he is writing remains incomplete, and when he hypothesizes about the missing final chapter, one that he says will be full of action, his outline of the next episode goes back on a circular route to the central chapter of the present book and to his paralysis and failure as he waits for H. de Heutz in the "funereal château where I lost my youth" (*PE*, p. 125). So, as one might expect in a study of ambiguity, though one may begin with assertions of similarity, one ends with finer and finer definitions of difference.

Notes

1. Patricia Smart, *Hubert Aquin, agent double* (Montréal: Presses de l'Université de Montréal, 1973), p.7. My translation.
2. *Liberté* 4 (Mai 1962): 299–325.
3. Hubert Aquin, *Prochain Episode*, trans. Penny Williams (Toronto: McClelland and Stewart, 1972), p. 9. Subsequent references will be cited as *PE*, followed by the page number, and enclosed in parentheses.
4. Ronald Sutherland, "Introduction," *Prochain Episode*, p.iv.
5. Ibid., p. viii.

8

Metamorphosis and Survival:
Notes on the Recent Poetry of Margaret Atwood

George Woodcock

"My purpose," says Ovid in the opening lines of *The Metamorphoses*, "is to tell of bodies which have been transformed into shapes of a different kind. You heavenly powers, since you were responsible for these changes, look favourably on my efforts."[1] And, as D. E. W. Wormell has remarked, Ovid, "With supreme skill . . . contrives a unity out of legends whose only point of contact is that all are concerned with change of shape."[2]

In Margaret Atwood's more recent books of verse, *You Are Happy* (1974), *Two-Headed Poems* (1978), and *True Stories* (1981), the theme of metamorphosis flows with remarkable strength, and even though she is not so consistent as Ovid in exemplifying it in all her late poems, it becomes a powerful uniting current. At one point, indeed, the paths of Ovid and Atwood cross, for Circe, perhaps inevitably, finds a place in the mythologies of both poets. Yet it is no more than a crossing, for Ovid is, like Virgil, directing his sequence of changes towards the foundation of Rome, and Circe enters as an incidental figure in the story of Aeneas. But Atwood is concerned with the story of Odysseus, whose encounter with Circe takes up a great deal of *You Are Happy*, and Odysseus was of course the universal survivor, the great resister of magic transformation though in another way one might call the *Odyssey* a western *Book of Changes*, for no poem tells more powerfully how the very struggle to sustain his true self against the assaults of experience changes a mortal hero steadily and irrevocably. As Atwood has it in the "Circe/Mud" cycle in *You Are Happy*:

> Your flawed body, sickle
> scars on the chest, moonmarks, the botched knee
> that nevertheless bends when you will it to

> Your body, broken and put together
> not perfectly, marred
> by war but moving
> despite that with such ease and leisure
>
> Your body that includes everything
> you have done, you have had done
> to you and goes beyond it.
>
> *(YAH*, p. 60)

In a past essay I found the essence of Atwood's earlier writings implied in one of the most concise and powerful poems of *Power Politics*:

> Beyond truth,
> tenacity: of those
> dwarf trees & mosses,
> hooked into straight rock
> believing the sun's lies & thus
> refuting/gravity
>
> & of this cactus, gathering
> itself together
> against the sand, yes tough
> rind & spikes but doing
> the best it can
>
> *(PP*, p. 36)

And I commented, in what I still feel is a valid summary of the most striking feature of Atwood's first decade of writing, whether in verse or prose:

> Here is not merely an attitude to life that is evident in all Atwood's writings —
> an attitude appropriate to an age when survival has become the great achievement. Here is also the metaphor that expresses a personal poetic, even a personal ethic. To be (tenacity) is more certain than to know (truth); one does the best one can, shapes one's verse like one's life to the improbable realities of existence ("the sun's lies"), and in this age and place the realities impose a defensive economy, poems close to the rock, poems spiny as cactuses or calthrops.[3]

But tenacity does not obviate change; it merely makes it slower and yet at the same time more irreversible, and even in Atwood's earlier writings the theme of change and the myth of metamorphosis are there, conveyed in powerful metaphors like the cake-woman in *The Edible Woman* which Marian MacAlpin eats in order to cure and transform herself, and in the submersion-surfacing imagery which accompanies the narrator's metamorphosis in *Surfacing* through a regression (magic transformation) into animality that heralds her move into a new level of understanding in a world of benign cosmic indifference, where "The Lake is quiet, the trees surround me, asking and giving nothing" (*Sfg*, p. 192). The poems are full of subtler images of change. Eskimo sculptures become the memories of shapes felt in the hand; the decay of totem poles makes them seem more living than the wooden people who look at them; strawberries in a dream garden turn into the blood that pioneers sweat.

Often change is used in these earlier poems to emphasize the continuity that is inescapable, the haunting survival of the past in the present it has become, as in the strange poem of the revenant Mrs. Moodie that ends *The Journals of Susanna Moodie*, "A Bus along St. Clair: December":

> It would take more than that to banish
> me: this is my kingdom still.
>
> Turn, look up
> through the gritty window: an unexplored
> wilderness of wires
>
> Though they buried me in monuments
> of concrete slabs, of cables
> though they mounded a pyramid
> of cold light over my head
> though they said, We will build
> silver paradise with a bulldozer
>
> it shows how little they know
> about vanishing: I have
> my ways of getting through.
>
> [. . .]
>
> Turn, look down:
> there is no city;
> this is the centre of a forest
>
> your place is empty.

(JSM, pp. 60-61)

But though the past permeates the present, the present hastens with ever greater speed into the future. This is another aspect of change that occurs in Atwood's earlier writing, nowhere more powerfully than in the extraordinary metamorphic poem that in *Power Politics* suddenly expands the private war between lovers into the universal war that is history. The perceiving persona who speaks throughout the book sees, almost cinematographically (as in a movie run at ever-increasing speed), the progression of feminine experience with herself as a kind of everlasting Penelope at the centre of it:

> At first I was given centuries
> to wait in caves, in leather
> tents, knowing you would never come back
>
> Then it speeded up: only
> several years between
> the day you jangled off
> into the mountains, and the day (it was
> spring again) I rose from the embroidery
> frame at the messenger's entrance.
>
> [. . .]
>
> But recently, the bad evenings
> there are only seconds
> between the warning on the radio and the
> explosion; my hands
> don't reach you
>
> and on quieter nights
> you jump up from
> your chair without even touching your dinner
> and I can scarcely kiss you goodbye
> before you run out into the street and they shoot

(PP, pp. 28–29)

This is a Penelope whose Odysseus never returns. "At first I was given centuries" in fact points forward to the poems preoccupied with the increasing atrocity of political relations in our time that play so important a part in Atwood's latest volume of verse, *True Stories*, published a decade after *Power Politics*. But it points forward to only one of the many ways in which metamorphosis, as metaphor and myth, has become perhaps the most important thematic element in Atwood's most recent poetry, and even her prose, for there are complex patterns of metamorphosis in a novel like *Lady Oracle*, though that lies beyond the purview of the present essay. As I shall show, this increasing emphasis on change and changes does not mean an abdication of Atwood's earlier preoccupation with survival, with the tenacity that lies beyond truth. But it does mean the development of a more fluid sense of the possibilities of the poet's own vision, accompanying and interacting with certain changes in her personal ambience that enter into the content of her poetry.

There is a haunting Imagist sufficiency about the title poem of *You Are Happy*; Imagism passes through practice into theory, as Atwood tells of a winter walk, beginning with a verse that is an irregular haiku: eighteen syllables arranged four, nine, five instead of seventeen arranged five, seven, five, but otherwise traditional in its natural image and seasonal setting:

> The water turns
> a long way down over the raw stone,
> ice crusts around it
>
> *(YAH*, p. 28)

The poem proceeds with the walk which the poet and her companion take, wandering to the open beach, seeing the unused picnic tables, the brown gravelly waves. The headless carcass of a deer lies in a ditch; a bird runs across the road in the pink glare of the low sun. All is stated in images, until the last five lines, which expound the very core of Imagist doctrine, the subordination of idea to image:

> When you are this
> cold you can think about
> nothing but the cold, the images
>
> hitting into your eyes
> like needles, crystals, you are happy.
>
> *(YAH*, p. 28)

Only in the very last phrase, "you are happy," is the emotion that the images have carried through the poem explicitly stated.

This poem exemplifies the startling actuality that is one of the striking features of so many of the items in *You Are Happy*. Such poems are related to the life which Atwood took up when in the early 1970's she retreated to live in old Loyalist country at Alliston, Ontario, in a way re-enacting Susanna Moodie's experiences, since she too was involved in a kind of pioneering, getting an old farm back into shape and some degree of production. They are poems about place, but unlike Al Purdy's poems about the Loyalist country, they are not really about time in the historic sense; Atwood is less concerned than Purdy about ancestors and prefers to find them in myth and literature rather than in the kind of genealogical speculation through which he pushes backward to the roots of our past, or at least of his.

It is living or reliving at most, rather than remembering, that is important in poems like "You Are Happy," or like "November," "Digging," and "Late August," in which the poet projects anew the images of country living that belong to the pioneer tradition rather than evoking the tradition itself.

The dead sheep found in "November" hangs in the barn as "a long fruit covered with wool and rotting" and becomes in the poet's mind "a legacy," out of which emerge the bitter maxims of the poem's final lines:

> Kill what you can't save
> what you can't eat throw out
> what you can't throw out bury
>
> What you can't bury give away
> what you can't give away you must carry with you,
> it is always heavier than you thought.

> (*YAH*, p. 17)

The past that is "always heavier than you thought" hangs like a miasma over "Digging," where the poet digs dung in the barnyard as if it were a way of exorcising anger, grudges, "old remorse." And when the exorcism has worked, there is the pure flame of experience, as in "You Are Happy," and the rich contentment of "Late August" that takes up the Keatsian theme — "Season of mists and mellow fruitfulness" — and makes out of it an exceptional Atwoodian poem in which the characteristic astringency is dissolved and a dreaming sensuality bridges the Romantic generations far more effectively than Keats's Canadian imitators did in the 1890's, with their precise metrical and metaphoric derivations. "Late August" is

> . . . the plum season, the nights
> blue and distended, the moon
> hazed, this is the season of peaches
>
> with their lush lobed bulbs
> that glow in the dusk, apples
> that drop and rot
> sweetly, their brown skins veined as glands

> [. . .]

> The air is still
> warm, flesh moves over
> flesh, there is no
>
> hurry

(YAH, p. 93)

There is a kind of verbal *trompe l'oeil* in such poems. Time and change seem to have been stilled: "there is no/hurry." And the illusion of timelessness is of course a quality of both Imagist poetry and of the kind of Romantic verse that was most strikingly exemplified in Keats's Odes. What is so clearly present is so in time, as well as space, and we have the sense of suspension in an eternal moment. But the very phrase, "eternal moment," gives the illusion away. Time starts up when we close the page, and we know that change has produced what the poet — and we vicariously — experience as changeless, and that change will afterwards break the spell. It is Atwood's acknowledgment of the co-existence of the sense of timelessness and changelessness that special times and moods confer on us, with the reality of change, that gives *You Are Happy* a range and a poignancy which make it more complex in its perplexities and its rewards than any of Atwood's earlier volumes.

The double core of the book is formed by the two groups of poems linked with the Circe myth in its Odyssean variant. Metamorphosis in the true Ovidian sense is the theme of the "Songs of the Transformed," sung by beasts who were men before they were changed by Circe. They stand before us in their bestial natures, speak in their animal voices, yet through the masks of their transformation they project the aspects of our humanity we normally conceal but which are now released because the deceptions by which we safeguard them are no longer needed. Thus, often in their final lines, the speakers in these poems make reflections that are totally and appallingly human in their implications, as when the pig declares:

> I am yours. If you feed me garbage,
> I will sing a song of garbage.
> This is a hymn.

(YAH, p. 30)

or the rat says:

> You'd do the same if you could,
>
> if you could afford to share
> my crystal hatreds.

(YAH, p. 32)

Or the crow remarks, in the voice of a tired leader:

> Watching you
> my people, I become cynical,
> you have defrauded me of hope
> and left me alone with politics . . .

(YAH, p. 34)

There is a difference between natural metamorphosis and magic transformation, and the more we read the "Songs of the Transformed," the more we realize that the change of appearance which has taken these creatures out of humanity has left unchanged the core of instinct which the relationships necessary to human society have modified and moralized. Turned into animals, men exhibit without inhibition the worst characteristics of the human beast, just as, when political or religious hysterias are deprived of their protective mutuality, men, who have not even grown fur or horns, will exhibit the negative traits which we call bestial but which in fact are more deeply human than we dare admit. In the later volume, *True Stories*, Margaret Atwood deals with the Circean monsters that still wear human masks.

"Songs of the Transformed" have to be read beside the "Circe/Mud Poems." Ostensibly this cycle of monologues that Circe addresses to Odysseus concerns, like *Power Politics*, the combination of need and conflict that dominates female-male relationships, but the implications run deeper.

The mud woman, crucial though she is, occupies only one poem of the cycle; a traveller told Circe that he and his friend constructed her in boyhood: "She began at the neck and ended at the knees and elbows; they stuck to the essentials." Making love to her soft moist body was ecstasy:

> His love for her was perfect, he could say anything to her, into her
> he spilled his entire life. She was swept away in a sudden flood.
> He said no woman since then has equalled her.

(YAH, p. 61)

Circe, in a way, is the equivalent of the mud woman, which is why they are linked in the title of the cycle. She owns the island and in a sense she *is* the island:

> This is mine, this island, you can have
> the rocks, the plants
> that spread themselves flat over
> the thin soil, I renounce them.

> You can have this water,
> this flesh, I abdicate.
>
> (*YAH*, p. 54)

And this is what gives her the powers. She is a manifestation of the earth mother. She names the island and what is on it, and to name is magically to control and to transform. "The fresh monsters are already breeding in my head." And she transforms men not into what they are not but into what, essentially, they are:

> I did not add the shaggy
> rugs, the tusked masks,
> they happened.
>
> (*YAH*, p. 48)

Her victims are transformed because they do not have the will to become more than they are, to change instead of being changed, whereas it is the will to say always "Onward," of which Circe accuses Odysseus, that saves him from her magic:

> You are impervious
> with hope, it hardens you,
> this joy, this expectation, gleams
> in your hand like axes
>
> (*YAH*, p. 53)

And because he has resisted transformation and remained his ever-changing self, the threat of departure is always there. As Circe says to him:

> "Don't evade, don't pretend you won't leave after all: you leave in the
> story and the story is ruthless."
>
> (*YAH*, p. 68)

The myth — the story "which is ruthless" — tells of Odysseus's departure. There are other islands to which he comes, and it is a poem about two islands, Circe's and another, that ends the "Circe/Mud Poems." On the first island *the events run themselves through / almost without us*" (*YAH*, p. 69). Magic transformations are predictable because they are always alike; they are the transformations that strip the human forms from men and women, and in other ways they will continue to haunt Margaret Atwood's later books, *Two-Headed Poems* and *True Stories*. But there is the other island:

The second I know nothing about
because it has never happened;

this land is not finished,
this body is not reversible.

(YAH, p. 69)

And this land which "is not finished" one can think of metaphorically as modern
life that has not yet made its own myths, or in a broad sense as Canada, or in a
narrow sense as the farm where the couple of the unmythical poems lives and
where the time is neither past nor future but always, imagistically, now:

We walk through a field, it is November,
the grass is yellow, tinged
with grey, the apples

are still on the trees,
they are orange, astonishing.

(YAH, pp. 69–70)

It is also a land where, as a later poem of *You Are Happy* says:

. . . we keep going,
fighting our ways, our way
not out but through.

(YAH, p. 76)

Two-Headed Poems seems like a strange oasis of relative calm between the
appalling mythical transformations that occupy so much of *You Are Happy* and the
horror of human atrocities grown habitual that cast such a shadow over *True
Stories*. I do not think there is any book by Atwood that is more tender in its tone
than this, or any in which one captures quite the same sense that it is good to be
alive and human, and that in some way, not heroic or spectacular, the manner in
which men live can make the world a little more than endurable. In *Two-Headed
Poems* the irony that in some of Atwood's earlier poems appears merely corrosive
becomes transformed into a kind of solvent of anger. The old theme of sexual
aggression, already relegated to the realm of legend in *You Are Happy*, is
diminished — reduced to the thought that "What defeats us . . . is / the repetition" *(THP,* p. 24).

It may be irrelevantly biographical to remark that the four years dividing *Two-
Headed Poems* from *You Are Happy* were a time of considerable literary success
for Margaret Atwood and to all appearances a time of greater personal happiness.

Yet the fact is that a sense of unexpected contentment is projected by the poems in the volume which are most closely linked to the actualities of a satisfying existence, largely dominated by Margaret Atwood's young daughter, whose presence, more than that of any other being, seems to dominate *Two-Headed Poems*. There are myths here, indeed, but they are something very near to folk myths, the myths of daily living, incorporated in such undramatic transformations as dolls or Hallowe'en heads made of paper bags, symbols whose very humbleness and indefiniteness give them more protean possibilities than the ritual magic of Circe with its permutations limited by tradition:

> Paper head, I prefer you
> because of your emptiness;
> from within you any
> word could still be said.
>
> With you I could have
> more than one skin,
> a blank interior, a repertoire
> of untold stories,
> a fresh beginning.
>
> (*THP*, p. 13)

Other, more sombre transformations do indeed appear in *Two-Headed Poems*; after all, it is a title that reminds us of Janus, the god of beginnings and endings, and the very first poem of the book — "Burned Space" — talks of the fundamental transformation that occurs when the timelessness of the natural cycle is dislocated by human intervention:

> Before the burn, this was a forest.
> Now it is something else:
>
> a burn twists the green
> eternal into singed grey
>
> history: these discarded
> stag-heads and small charred bones.
>
> (*THP*, pp. 8–9)

The statement is environmental propaganda; the poem is art. Perhaps the elegiac is the only mood that can be didactic and at the same time poetic.

There are two cycles within *Two-Headed Poems* entitled "Daybooks." My first reaction when I read them was to think of Robert Frost; like so many of Frost's poems, they seemed to me concrete and suggestive notations on country living. But in fact, without ceasing to resemble Frost, they are nearer to Hesiod's *Works and Days*, with the strange combination one finds in those archaic Greek poems of a realistic sense of the difficulties of country life with an awareness of the emotional sustenance that is also a part of rural living. One of the most appealing poems in the "Daybooks" cycles is "Apple Jelly," which describes and decorates, and at the same time celebrates, opening out to a generous mood of awareness and acceptance that is far different from the tight simplicities of *Power Politics* and other poems of earlier periods:

> No sense in all this picking,
> peeling & simmering
> if sheer food is all
> you want; you can buy it cheaper.
>
> Why then do we burn our hours
> & muscles in this stove,
> cut our thumbs, to get these tiny
> glass pots of clear jelly?
>
> Hoarded in winter: the sun
> on that noon, your awkward leap
> down from the tree,
> licked fingers, sweet pink juice,
> what we keep
> the taste of the act, taste
> of this day.

(*THP*, p. 93)

Sometimes the remembered taste of country life has, as in Hesiod, a bitterness quite different from the winter sweetness of apple jelly; yet in the end, as another poem, "Nothing New Here," declares, there is a frugal compensation that Hesiod would appreciate:

> (. . . this broken
> garden, measure
> of our neglect and failure, still
> gives what we eat.)

(*THP*, p. 25)

There is here, once again, tenacity, that recurrent alternative *leitmotif* of Atwood's writing.

There are also items in *Two-Headed Poems*, such as "Footnote to the Amnesty Report on Torture" and "Marrying the Hangman," that carry the darker vision of human potentialities through from the earlier volumes towards *True Stories*. But there is as well, at times, a deep sense of the underlying and continuing community of mankind, expressed with particular eloquence in that epiphany of a poem, "The Bus to Alliston, Ontario":

> Outside, the moon is fossil
> white, the sky cold purple, the stars
> steely and hard; when there are trees they are dried
> coral; the snow
> is an unbroken spacelit
> desert through which we make
> our ordinary voyage,
> those who hear voices and those
> who do not, moving together, warm
> and for the moment safe,
> along the invisible road towards home.
>
> (*THP*, p. 78)

It is appropriate that *Two-Headed Poems* should be, as well as everything else, a lesson in existence. In "You Begin," the poet is talking to her daughter, starting with images, things, colours, words, the stuff of poetry, and coming to man's primordial and distinguishing gift, the hand:

> The word *hand* anchors
> your hand to this table,
> your hand is a warm stone
> I hold between two words.
>
> This is your hand, these are my hands, this is the world,
> which is round but not flat and has more colours
> than we see.
>
> It begins, it has an end,
> this is what you will
> come back to, this is your hand.
>
> (*THP*, p. 111)

True Stories, appearing in 1981, seven years after *You Are Happy*, represents the end of a cycle, and on the personal and the physical level it is all summed up in the poem "High Summer":

Goodbye, we credit

the apple trees, dead
and alive, with saying.

They say no such thing.

(TS, p. 102)

Reading this poem, one is aware that there are no claims made; the past is not insistent, as it is in Purdy's poems about the same countryside. The sense of a liaison between the land and its inhabitants that other poets might seek to induce is not acknowledged. The myth, the story we invent for our own solace and protection, is meaningless except to its inventors, we are told. But so also is the "true" story that pretends to be the opposite of myth, as the title poem tells us:

The true story is vicious
and multiple and untrue

after all. Why do you
need it? Don't ever

ask for the true story.

(TS, p. 11)

Yet much of *True Stories* in fact consists of a kind of poetic actuality, a continuing oblique comment on the world that is our here and now. Poetically, in my view, it is the best verse Atwood has yet written, honed down to a stark directness, an accuracy of sound, yet always lit with that visual luminosity and sharpness which make poetry more than a mere verbal exercise, a Swinburnian patterning of sound. And it tells us, once again, after the relatively benign interlude of *Two-Headed Poems*, not only of the abdication of reason suggested in the title poem, but also of the tyranny of the senses and the cruel proximity of violence and love.

One of the striking aspects of *True Stories*, which it shares with much of *Two-Headed Poems*, is the metaphoric process by which thoughts merge into sensations, so that the mind seems imprisoned in its flesh, yet things in a curious and compensating way become liberated into thought, so that a landcrab is not only its hard evasive self but also a concept:

> . . . a piece of what
> we are, not all,
> my stunted child, my momentary
> face in the mirror,
> my tiny nightmare.
>
> (*TS*, p. 13)

And even though in a sequel, "Landcrab II," the poet remarks, "You're no-one's metaphor," it is the previous concept that stays in the mind, just as a longish poem later in the book called "Mushrooms" builds up inevitably to the final unknotting of a metaphor:

> Here is the handful
> of shadow I have brought back to you:
> this decay, this hope, this mouth-
> ful of dirt, this poetry.
>
> (*TS*, p. 93)

This constant interplay between the sensual and the intellectual, between things and thoughts, provides the formal remoteness from which Atwood, like Auden's *Just*, can exchange her messages. For these are poems that, even while they warn us not to rely too much on reason — even our own reason — are nevertheless saying factual things about the world in which love exists — but also survives — on sufferance, threatened by the kinds of violence and injustice that none of our civilized theories or codes of conduct can comprehend.

The poems assembled in the middle section of *True Stories* — "Notes Towards A Poem That Can Never Be Written" — read often like a verse abtract of the more harrowing sections of Amnesty International reports. They too are poems of metamorphosis, of the frightful transformations, without magic, that the malign human intelligence can alone invent.

> . . . I think of the woman
> they did not kill.
> Instead they sewed her face
> shut, closed her mouth
> to a hole the size of a straw,
> and put her back on the streets,
> a mute symbol.
>
> (*TS*, p. 50)

These poems depict a condition of unreasoning barbarity, where cruelty and death are no longer tragic but merely gratuitous, absurd in their horror.

> . . . you're unable
> to shake the concept of tragedy,
> that what one gets
> is what's deserved, more
> or less; that there's a plot
> and innocence is merely
> not to act.
>
> (*TS*, p. 49)

It is no longer a world for taking sides, since "such things are done as soon as there are sides."

Perhaps the most appalling thing of all, in this world as Atwood contemplates it, is the way cruelty can shift into disarming kindness — after Hitler's war the waiter in the Vienna-Bonn express can still give "a purple egg to my child / for fun" — and we are faced with the "old fear" about ourselves:

> not what can be done to you
> but what you might do
> yourself, or fail to.
>
> This is the old torture.
>
> (*TS*, p. 61)

These poems may not — cannot — portray the rational, since they are concerned with areas of human existence from which reason has abdicated. Yet in themselves they are rational. They are also, taken together, one of the most intensely moral pieces of writing I have read in recent years, and no less so because they savage romantic notions of love, motherhood, and so on, and show how much myths can imprison and, indeed, destroy.

Yet *True Stories* is not all negation; its very moral intensity makes that impossible. It is about human cruelty and about human love, yet the two are far less fatally intertwined than they were in earlier Atwood poetry, like *Power Politics*. Cruelty is immediate and, at its worst, impersonal; love is a longing over distances, as in the earlier poems of *True Stories*, which are set on a Caribbean island.

> . . . Love comes
> in waves like the ocean, a sickness which goes on
> & on, a hollow cave
> in the head, filling & pounding, a kicked ear.
>
> (*TS*, p. 19)

It is also a necessary contradiction to a world of violence. In "Small Poems for the Winter Solstice," the speaker asks her lover:

> . . . How can I justify
> this gentle poem then in the face of sheer
> horror?
>
> (*TS*, p. 34)

And she answers her own question: "I know you by your / opposites." It is through the presence of the opposites that we endure. The last lines of "Last Day" — the last lines of the book — are an image of renewal.

> . . . This egg
> in my hand is our last meal,
> you break it open and the sky
> turns orange again and the sun rises
> again and this is the last day again.
>
> (*TS*, p.103)

There are, in my view, a number of criteria of poetic excellence that apply, especially in our time, in addition to a compulsive devotion to expression in verse: intense visual awareness; sharp verbal accuracy that makes, to adapt Orwell's metaphor, verse like a windowpane; deep moral sensitivity; the intuitive wisdom that in the last resort will accept the irrational as truer than the rational. Atwood, as her most recent volumes have shown, has all these qualities in abundance. She has also the over-reaching vision without which such qualities would in isolation be ineffective. Seen from this point in her life, her work — in prose and verse alike — presents a unity that reflects her dominant themes, tenacious survival and constant metamorphosis.

Notes

1. Ovid, *The Metamorphoses*, trans. Mary M. Innes (Harmondsworth: Penguin Books, 1955), p. 31.
2. D. R. Dudley and D. M. Lang, ed., *Penguin Companion to Literature* (Harmondsworth: Penguin Books, 1969), v. 4: p. 127.
3. George Woodcock, *The World of Canadian Writing* (Vancouver: Douglas and McIntyre, 1980), p. 158.

9

Atwood In A Landscape

Lorraine Weir

It is comforting, however, and a source of profound relief to think that man is only a recent invention, a figure not yet two centuries old, a new wrinkle in our knowledge, and that he will disappear again as soon as that knowledge has discovered a new form.

Michel Foucault

What follows is a series of afterwords, reflections on the manifold question of landscape, language, text, body — their meaning, relationships, congruence, and conflict in Atwood. It is a contribution to a hermeneutics of this place from which we speak, this place which a humanist tradition has taught us to define and thus perceive as "landscape" and which Atwood's work moves through and teaches us to experience in very different ways.

"Literature," Atwood writes in *Survival,* "is not only a mirror; it is also a map, a geography of the mind" (*Sur*, pp. 18–19). Both maps and literary works constitute a people's "shared knowledge" of their place; both create community and become enactments of mirroring rites creative of place in terms of both self and world. Literature is topography but, to paraphrase Derrida,[1] what is a text, and what must topography be if it can be represented by a text?

1. TÓPOS/GRÁPHEIN

This is border country.

(*Sfg*, p. 26)

Topography is literally the writing of a place, a *tópos*. Traditional rhetoric asserts the equivalence of *tópos* and *locus*, rhetorical "places," topics embroidered as foci in situations of formal public discourse. In the practice of *ars memoria*, the speaker "placed" his memory *loci* in convenient locations around the site of his oration, enabling him to retrieve elements of his discourse as he glanced about him.[2] Similarly, the writing of places situates them within a rhetorical space, the space of discourse, rendering place textual. The codes of map-making, like all codes, must then be shared, participatory, lest the map and thus the *tópos* become a solipsism. In the case of topography, writing seems to ensure this commonality. It seems to assert the centrality of reader in text, the centrality of place in writing. In fact, "it is difficult to imagine that access to the possibility of a road-map is not at the same time access to writing."[3]

But what if the relationship of easy reciprocity implicit in this statement is not the case? What if the space of writing and of place are not shared; what if the writing of place is but the assertion of a false centrality on the part of the writer?

> Man *calls himself* man only by drawing limits excluding his other from the play of supplementarity: the purity of nature, of animality, primitivism, childhood, madness, divinity. The approach to these limits is at once feared as a threat to death, and desired as access to a life without differance. The history of man *calling himself* man is the articulation of *all* these limits among themselves . . . Writing will appear to us more and more as another name for this structure of supplementarity.[4]

Or, as Charles Darwin put part of it, "If man had not been his own classifier, he would never have thought of founding a separate order for his own reception."[5]

Aligned with the metaphysics of "presence," the concept of the supplement for Derrida indicates that to which man points in the assertion of his otherness before both the rest of creation and the notion of a creator. Seeking to bind up the wound of guilt and of impending death, man locates himself within a world of his own devising, thereby displacing writing into the realm of transcendence. The violence of writing, in turn, imposes a humanist valorization upon the world, dividing the human from the non-human, the civilized from the savage, the part from the whole, the road from the land. This is what Derrida calls "differance," the creation of the humanist cosmos in which "The *silva* is savage, the *via rupta* is written, discerned, and inscribed violently as difference, as form imposed on the *hylè*, in the forest, in wood as matter."[6] Thus the writing of places divides man from "his" world, creates ownership even as it imposes "order," ironically creates metaphysical "presence" even as it jettisons man from the ecosphere and — as though in compensation — sustains the delusion of human supremacy in a world apparently designed for our consumption.

In "border country," the deception becomes obvious.

2. ALCHERINGA

> In truth we are always already at home in language, just as much as we are in
> the world.
>
> Hans-Georg Gadamer

Alcheringa is the "dream-time" sacred to the Australian aboriginal peoples. To
enter this sacred space is to enter the possibility of experiencing what Paul Ricoeur
has referred to as the fundamental unity of the ground of being, a unitary system
enfolding man and nature, past and present, within which meaning is encoded. It
is grounded in an understanding of human oneness with the non-human and of the
possibility of entering synchronic time in which, through repetition of the founding gestures and mysteries of Baiamai, the sacred time of the beginning is
reintegrated with the present. Similarly, Mircea Eliade suggests that settlement in
a new territiory is mythically resolved into ritual repetition of this process of
transforming chaos into cosmos[7] which is celebrated in the rituals of *Alcheringa*.
In Atwood, however, this homology is split.

This can best be demonstrated by contrasting these structures in two representative texts, "Progressive Insanities of a Pioneer" and *Surfacing*. In the former, the
pioneer's attempted transformation of chaos into cosmos or of "unstructured
space" into "order" results finally in the invasion of "the green / vision" (*AC*, p.
39). Opposed to this vision is the "green paper" from which the pioneer in the
beginning "proclaim[ed] himself the centre," setting up a relationship of opposition between himself conceived as subject and the land conceived as object.
Opposition takes two analogous forms: the attempted transformation of soil into
furrows and of "nowhere" into place, "nameless" weeds into named "Things."
It is a topographic exercise in which the *tópoi* themselves condition defeat, single
insanities initiated by an error in vocabulary representative of a worldview in
which "progress" is generated by the hubris of valorizing self over against and at
the expense of ecosphere. This failure of recognition is signalled in part through
the use of "aqueous language"[8] which, from *Power Politics* until *Surfacing*,
denotes the unitary cosmology associated with Ojibwa tradition in the latter.

Insanity, the narrator of *Surfacing* says, is speaking a language which no one
else understands (*Sfg*, p. 190). The pioneer speaks the language of humanist
presumption and is answered out of the aphoristic speech of *Alcheringa*. His ritual
of origination is rejected by the land — a rejection of textuality centred in the
violence of writing. Shovels are pens in this writing: they introduce chaos into

cosmos rather than transforming it. Entry is refused until mutuality of understanding is achieved which, in turn, requires the pioneer to acknowledge the world, to comprehend that his judgment of "nowhere" constitutes an act of bad faith. In terms of *Surfacing* this is the awareness which Joe must come to — and in which the narrator makes an explicit act of faith at the end of her quest — that he has been complicit in "Americanism," the "random sampling" of self and world.

But the status of world is itself in question.

3. EARTH/WORLD

> In setting up a world, the work sets forth the earth . . . The work moves the earth itself into the Open of a world and keeps it there. *The work lets the earth be an earth.*
>
> Martin Heidegger

In "The Origin of the Work of Art," Martin Heidegger situates the work of art, or what I will refer to here as the text, within the striving of world and earth. "The *world worlds*," Heidegger writes,

> and is more fully in being than the tangible and perceptible realm in which we believe ourselves to be at home. World is never an object that stands before us and can be seen. World is the ever-nonobjective to which we are subject as long as the paths of birth and death, blessing and curse keep us transported into Being. Wherever those decisions of our history that relate to our very being are made, are taken up and abandoned by us, go unrecognized and are rediscovered by new inquiry, there the world worlds.[9]

World is "self-opening." Earth, on the other hand, is "the spontaneous forthcoming of that which is continually self-secluding and to that extent sheltering and concealing." In striving against one another, earth and world are united in what Heidegger refers to as "the intimacy of simple belonging to one another," for "The world grounds itself on the earth, and earth juts through world."[10] The text both "instigates" and "accomplishes" this striving. It is a thing expressed by world, opening into earth and thus both a sign of world's violence and a vehicle of earth's "presencing." The text itself is then a striving. Through its violence comes what Roland Barthes calls "bliss."[11] The bliss of the text is the revelation of earth's unconcealedness.

World's striving is the "technosphere."[12] Motivated by a politics of individual gain secure in the conviction that "*Tout est créé pour l'homme,*"[13] the technosphere in the post-Heideggerian universe encounters the ecosphere and striving becomes exploitation, finally destruction. Again in Atwood the paradigm is a binary one, for in *Surfacing* the "bliss of the text" results from the resolution of the tension between opposites ("Americanism" in all its forms, and the vision quest) on the one hand and, on the other, the first full expression in the Atwood system of the cosmology which will resolve the tension inherent in the verbal and visual codes denoted in the poetry before *Two-Headed Poems and Others*[14] by semantic and thematic operations of enclosure and disclosure.

Or, to put it another way, only the text of flesh may encounter earth.

Word is the bond of earth and world within what Heidegger calls the "Open" of the text, but in Atwood this is the bond not of technosphere and ecosphere striving in intimacy (the idealist yearning toward a "value-free" science) but of those "savage fields" transcended within the text. This is the movement which is presented first in proleptic form in *Surfacing* and fully in *Two-Headed Poems and Others*. Both texts trace ways of living within the eschaton. Thus a post-Heideggerian understanding of earth/world striving as explicit and deadly strife (which Dennis Lee summarizes under the heading "planet"[15]) is balanced in Atwood against a dual apprehension of the earth-dwelling of the work of art and the earth-affirmation of the unitary cosmology — *Alcheringa*, the vision quest, the shamanic tradition.

That this affirmation is grounded in a firm rejection of the humanist "mystification" of man is clear.[16] Consonant with this position is a denial of the possibility of authenticity to language/writing rooted in the technosphere and in its values — the world to which *Surfacing's* concept of Americanism stands in metonymic relation. The mid-point of this linguistic transformation process for *Surfacing's* narrator, the encounter with the Ojibwa pictographs (both in her father's drawings of them and, seemingly, in the original), reflects both her freedom in the middle of the vision quest from the false language and values of the technosphere, and her journey toward silence at the apogee of the quest. Silence is the beginning of authentic language, unfiltered memory, the vision of earth. Further, if the pictographs are viewed as icons from the Ojibwa creation scrolls, used by their shamanic owners in rituals of origination as mnemonic devices (rhetorical *loci* or *tópoi*) together with sacred lore and shamanic dream,[17] then the narrator may be seen to be replicating their traditional function. In their concentration of power on the edge of speech, in their taut resolution in gnomic form of the knowledge of a people, resides the power of the pictographs for her. Defying "reading," pictographs exist on the border of revelation, accessible — like the figure of the heron — only to those who have left world and assented to earth, to the integration of the human with the non-human, to an ethic of participation rather than of domination. Like the heron, they assert the reality of meaning even in the gash of world's "worlding."

4. AFTER JAYNES

> . . . the world burns.
>
> (*THP*, p. 111)
>
> . . . decolonization is always a violent phenomenon.
>
> Frantz Fanon

"The nervous systems of poets come like shoes, in all types and sizes, though with a certain irreducible typology":[18] thus Julian Jaynes concludes his discussion of poets and bicamerality in *The Origin of Consciousness in the Breakdown of the Bicameral Mind*, one of the texts of violence at the centre of *Two-Headed Poems and Others*. Like the heads of Atwood's Siamese twins, the voices of Jaynes' book "speak sometimes singly, sometimes together" (*THP*, p. 59), manifesting both the logic of the technosphere in application to *Alcheringa* and the nostalgia of the technocrat in search of undemanding, occasional gods. His theory is simple, not to say simplistic: consciousness or the "analog 'I'," [19] the self-reflexive voice, is the product of a radical shift in human neurophysiology which resulted in the dwindling of the "bicameral mind." Religious man was — and, to the extent that he survives for Jaynes, is — a bicameral being, which is to say that he experienced in a direct fashion, most frequently through auditory hallucinations, the voices of his gods. Pre-reflective man, as yet unable to distance himself from the moment and thus establish an awareness of self as distinct from other or from environment, lived out of the "god-side" [20] or right temporal lobe of his brain, experiencing visions, voices, and poems just as — so Jaynes argues — the modern schizophrenic does. With the coming of consciousness or reflective capacity — the activation of the "man-side" or left temporal hemisphere of the brain — came the rise of technology and the death of the gods.

Thus for Jaynes poets and madmen are alike. Their "irreducible typology" results from bicameral dominance, their right hemispheres still functioning powerfully in a left-dominant world. The struggle of the right and the left is, then, the strife of earth and world met in post-Heideggerian violence. Battling for control of the planet and of bodies and texts, the right and the left — with left as technosphere maintaining dominance — encounter each other on the field of language. Retracing the evolution of words, the combatants move back through verbs to names and then nouns. And since, for Jaynes as for Giambattista Vico, with names came graves, this movement through language becomes also an encounter with death.

Jaynes' theory provides the overture to the struggle of left and right in *Two-Headed Poems and Others*. On the one hand is the technocrat's literalization of the modes and values of *Alcheringa*. On the other is a much more complex process of transformation involving the purgation of this literalization which is the violence done to earth, to the text of flesh. Preparatory to the transformation of blood into bread (*THP*, p. 109), an understanding of world's violence must be achieved. This necessitates passage through world, the "man-side" of the brain, and the experience of its voices and false logic. Thus, like the vision quest in *Surfacing*, the struggle of left and right in *Two-Headed Poems* centres on the encounter with blood and, moving through the stages of what Heidegger calls "World-withdrawal and world-decay,"[21] emerges again into the proclamation of the unitary cosmology.

Where death in *The Journals of Susanna Moodie* is the empty transcendence of being equally without language and without flesh, in *Two-Headed Poems* it is incorporated in bread — the balance of "Live burial," "white famine bellies," and "lungfuls of warm breath stopped / in the heat from an old sun" against breaking, sharing, and the knowledge which is consecration (*THP*, pp. 108–9). Against consecration is balanced torture; against the ritual gestures of making clothes and food, the encounter with fear and incapacity in old age and with the "locked room" of a marriage which is a prison (*THP*, p. 51); against the "Burned Space" of earth which is both the burning of forest and of skin ("after a burn / your hands are never the same" *THP* p. 9) is the burning of the world with colour, prelude to the laying on of hands which is language ("your hand is a warm stone / I hold between two words" — *THP*, p. 111). To *be* alive is to be force-fed with nouns (*THP*, p. 74); to *choose* life is to understand that

> Language, like the mouths
> that hold and release
> it, is wet & living, each
>
> word is wrinkled
> with age, swollen
> with other words, with blood, smoothed by the numberless
> flesh tongues that have passed across it.
>
> (*THP*, p. 67)

This is the voice of the "god-side," the voice of earth. The other side, world's voice, knows that "each word is empire, / each word is vampire and mother" for to be drained of the blood of language (the blood which is the bliss of the text *in potentia*, the claim of language upon the body) is to be capable of colonization. The right side is the sphere of the mother, the teaching of language; the left is the sphere of technocracy, the trapping of words (*THP*, p. 68). Between them is the language of "double-think": "As for the sun, there are as many / suns as there are words for sun; / false or true?" (*THP*, p. 67)

. . . false in a book in which the rhythm of dozens of declarative sentences defining what "is" insists upon the power and claim of language uttered in good faith to name the earth and define the space of world. But, like the ordeals necessary to the accomplishment of the vision quest in *Surfacing*, the journey through the purgatory of linguistic ambivalence and the violence of writing with its assertion of human territoriality (*tópos/gráphein*) is essential to the assertion of the place of naming which concludes both *Two-Headed Poems* and *Surfacing*. The "message from the flayed tongue / to the flayed ear"[22] is the refusal of two-headedness which, like Klee's "Senecio," sees neither left nor right but only strife and obfuscation. It is the message that beyond a technosphere which seeks to encapsulate the text in limitation — to colonize it,   "nobody owns the earth."[23]

5. BUILDING/DWELLING/COMMUNITAS

> Only if we are capable of dwelling, only then can we build.
>
>   Martin Heidegger

To build, for Heidegger, is to join the spaces of a place. "The nature of building is letting dwell,"[24] for both earth and man must open into the work, must share in the movement toward dwelling. Dwelling is *"the basic character* of Being in keeping with which mortals exist";[25] it is the choice again and again of the text of flesh over that of violence, the consecration of blood and ashes in the eating of earth. And that "sparing and preserving" which Heidegger states is the fundamental character of dwelling[26] is equally the sparing and preserving of that which is most deeply human and of earth mediated not by world, the assertion of man, but by the text of flesh, the body's capacity for earth-dwelling. It is the refusal to draw limits, the refusal to experience guilt in the imperfect gesture, in the ordinariness of daily living, in the dwindling of a life, for "At bottom, the ordinary is not ordinary; it is extra-ordinary, uncanny."[27] And, in *Two-Headed Poems*, it is the redefinition of mimesis, rejected in the earlier collections of poems in its association with the technosphere and its traditions, in the warping of earth by world. In passing through blood, we move beyond the violence of mirrors.

Redefined here, too, is the earlier dyadic relationship between the poles of transcendence and limitation in association with earth and world. In a movement homologous to that of the narrator of *Surfacing*, liminality is taken as vehicle of communitas, which is to say, after Victor Turner, that those who exist on the margin of a structure move through transgression of its codes and norms into an apprehension of the sacred, *"das Zwischenmenschliche."*[28] Or, to use Atwood's codes, it is the redefinition of the verbal code of eye and word as mediated by hands and hearts, the code of place which opens into dwelling and flesh.

But the system is still one whose shamans are women and whose experience of communitas is centred in what Robin Morgan refers to as "matriheritage."[29] "Sons branch out, but / one woman leads to another" (*THP*, p. 37). Along the "long thread of red blood" (*THP*, p. 103) move the stories which transmit language as garment of both protection and transformation from mother to daughter, from one woman to another (*THP*, p. 49). It is history given in stones (*THP*, p. 90) and in bones, in the elegiac movement back through the "old bone / tunnel" (*THP*, p. 40) to the voice of a shell which

> . . . was once filled with whispers;
> it was once a horn
> you could blow like a shaman
> conjuring the year,
> and your children would come running.

(*THP*, p. 33)

Conjuring, like the shell itself, is an opening into earth, a moving through blood to discover not only the world's burning but the taste of earth as well.

Notes

Sources of the epigraphs in the order in which they appear in the paper are as follows:

Michel Foucault *The Order of Things* (London: Tavistock, 1970), p. xxiii.

Hans-Georg Gadamer "Man and Language," in *Philosophical Hermeneutics*, trans. & ed. David E. Linge (Berkeley: University of California Press, 1976), p. 63.

Martin Heidegger "The Origin of the Work of Art," in *Poetry, Language, Thought*, trans. Albert Hofstadter (N.Y.: Harper Colophon, 1975), p. 46. Heidegger's emphasis.

Frantz Fanon *The Wretched of the Earth*, trans. Constance Farrington (N.Y.: Grove Press, 1968), p. 35.

Martin Heidegger "Building Dwelling Thinking," in *Poetry, Language, Thought*, p. 160.

1. Jacques Derrida, "Freud and the Scene of Writing," in *Writing and Difference*, trans. Alan Bass (Chicago: University of Chicago Press, 1978), p. 199.
2. See Frances Yates, *The Art of Memory* (Harmondsworth: Peregrine, 1969).
3. Jacques Derrida, *Of Grammatology*, trans. Gayatri Chakravorty Spivak (Baltimore: Johns Hopkins University Press, 1976), pp. 107–8.
4. Ibid., pp. 244–45. Derrida's emphasis.
5. Quoted by Kenneth Burke, "Order, Action, and Victimage," in *The Concept of Order*, ed. Paul G. Kuntz (Seattle: University of Washington Press, 1968), p. 170.
6. Derrida, *Of Grammatology*, p. 108.
7. Mircea Eliade, *The Myth of the Eternal Return*, trans. Willard R. Trask (Princeton: Princeton University Press, 1971), p. 10. On *Alcheringa*, see W. E. H. Stanner, "The Dreaming," in *Reader in Comparative Religion: An Anthropological Approach*, ed. William A. Lessa and Evon Z. Vogt (N.Y.: Harper and Row, 1958), pp. 158–67. On the Ojibwa unitary cosmology and its relevance to *Surfacing*, see Marie-Françoise Guédon's essay in this volume. I take Guédon's argument as given throughout this paper. *Alcheringa* has been used here not because I wish to argue any direct Australian influence on Atwood's system but rather because it seems to me the most inclusive and

accessible form of that state which is represented in Ojibwa cosmology only in its malign form, that of the Bearwalk (See Selwyn Dewdney, *The Sacred Scrolls of the Southern Ojibway* [Toronto: University of Toronto Press, 1975], pp. 116–18).

8. On "aqueous language" and its significance in Atwood's poetry, see Lorraine Weir, "Meridians of Perception: A Reading of Margaret Atwood's Poetry," in *The Art of Margaret Atwood*, ed. A. and C. Davidson (Toronto: Anansi, 1980), pp. 69–79.
9. Heidegger, *Poetry, Language, Thought*, pp. 44–45. Heidegger's emphasis.
10. Ibid., pp. 48–49.
11. Roland Barthes, *The Pleasure of the Text*, trans. Richard Miller (N.Y.: Hill and Wang, 1975).
12. On "technosphere," "ecosphere," and the scientific and political underpinnings of the unitary cosmology, see Barbara Ward and René Dubos, *Only One Earth — The Care and Maintenance of a Small Planet* (N.Y.: Norton, 1972).
13. This is A. O. Lovejoy's summary statement of the "Chain of Being" in eighteenth-century thought (see A. O. Lovejoy, *The Great Chain of Being* [Cambridge, MA.: Harvard University Press, 1961], p. 186).
14. On these codes and operations, see Lorraine Weir, "Meridians of Perception."
15. My debt to Dennis Lee's study, *Savage Fields — An Essay in Literature and Cosmology* (Toronto: Anansi, 1977) will be obvious throughout this section though my use of Heidegger in application to Atwood results in different emphases from Lee's work on Ondaatje and Cohen. While Lee and I agree that in the post-Heideggerian universe, "earth" and "world" are in violent conflict, his readings of Ondaatje and Cohen lead him to assert the absolute nature of that conflict at this point in history. However, it seems to me that Atwood's system provides at least a partial solution to the problem of savage fields through meticulous analysis and radical critique of that state and its effects (as Barbara Blakely's essay in this volume demonstrates) as well as presenting in *Surfacing* a transformative strategy which (as Marie-Françoise Guédon's essay makes clear) is much more profound in its implications than has previously been recognized.
16. Or, as Paul Ricoeur puts it, "The claim of some to demystify . . . speech and saying ought itself to be demystified, as being noncritical and naive" ("Structure, Word, Event," in *The Conflict of Interpretations*, ed. Don Ihde [Evanston: Northwestern University Press, 1974], p. 85). Cf. Eli Mandel's essay in this volume.
17. See Selwyn Dewdney, *Sacred Scrolls*, p. 22 and *passim*.
18. Julian Jaynes, *The Origin of Consciousness in the Breakdown of the Bicameral Mind* (Boston: Houghton Mifflin, 1977), p. 376. Thanks are due to my student, Sandy McIlwain, for getting me to read Jaynes sooner than I had intended to.
19. Ibid., p. 65.
20. Ibid., pp. 107–17.
21. Heidegger, *Poetry, Language, and Thought*, p. 41.
22. "After Jaynes," *THP*, p. 31. This poem refers to the custom, described in Jaynes, of decapitating deceased rulers and preserving their heads. Precious stones were set in the eye sockets and the heads were placed in sacred repositories from which, according to Jaynes' theory, they were heard by their subjects to speak with the voices of gods (*Origin of Consciousness*, pp. 169–75 and *passim*). Readers interested in source/influence study with reference to Atwood will find much to work with in Jaynes. My intention here is not primarily to explore his book in that way but rather to use Jaynes in thinking about the Atwood system and responding to it through philosophical systems which seem to me to open the work out.
23. Bill Bissett, *Nobody owns the earth* (Toronto: Anansi, 1971).
24. Martin Heidegger, "Building Dwelling Thinking," p. 160.
25. Ibid., Heidegger's emphasis.
26. Ibid., p. 149.
27. Heidegger, "The Origin of the Work of Art," p. 54.
28. Victor Turner, *The Ritual Process — Structure and Anti-Structure* (Ithaca: Cornell University Press, 1977), p. 136, quoting Martin Buber. In a further quotation from Buber, Turner defines communitas as "the being no longer side by side (and . . . above and below) but *with* one another of a multitude of persons. And this multitude, though it moves towards one goal, yet experiences everywhere a turning to, a dynamic facing of, the others, a flowing from *I* to *Thou*" (p. 127,

Buber's emphasis). See "Liminality and Communitas" and "Communitas: Model and Process" (ibid., pp. 94–165).

29. Robin Morgan, "The Network of the Imaginary Mother," in *Lady of the Beasts* (N.Y.: Random House, 1962), p. 66.

Notes on Contributors

BARBARA BLAKELY is an Anglican priest. She has lectured in the Women's Studies programmes at Simon Fraser University and the University of British Columbia. Her research interests are in the development of a feminist phenomenology, and she is currently working on a phenomenological, psychoanalytic, and materialist analysis of the position of women in myth and in religious systems.

ROBERT CLUETT is Professor of English and Director of the Graduate Programme in English at York University. He has published a number of computer-assisted analyses and is the author of *Prose Style and Critical Reading* (1976).

SHERRILL E. GRACE is Associate Professor of English at the University of British Columbia. She has published articles on Modern and Canadian subjects and is the author of the Introduction to the 1978 Anansi reprint of *The Circle Game*, of *Violent Duality: A Study of Margaret Atwood* (1980) and *The Voyage That Never Ends: Malcolm Lowry's Fiction* (1982). She is currently working on Expressionism in North American literature.

MARIE-FRANÇOISE GUÉDON is Assistant Professor of Anthropology at the University of British Columbia and former member of the Canadian Ethnology Service of the National Museum of Man. She has published ethnographic studies of Athapaskan and Tsimshian shamanism and a book, *People of Tetlin, Why are You Singing?* (1974).

LINDA HUTCHEON is Associate Professor of English at McMaster University and Adjunct Professor at the Centre for Comparative Literature, University of Toronto. She has published articles on contemporary Canadian literature and is the author of *Narcissistic Narrative: The Metafictional Paradox* (1980) and *Empirical Aesthetics: Charles Mauron, Roger Fry, Sigmund Freud* (1982).

ELI   MANDEL is Professor of English and Humanities at York University. Among his critical writings are *Criticism: Silent-Speaking Worlds* (1967) and *Another Time* (1977). His most recent publications are *Dreaming Backwards, Collected Poetry 1954-1981* (1981) and *Life Sentence Poems and Journals, 1976-1980* (1981). In 1982 Professor Mandel was made a Fellow of the Royal Society of Canada.

PHILIP STRATFORD is Professor of English at Université de Montréal. Among his books are *Faith and Fiction: Creative Process in Greene and Mauriac* (1964) and *Marie-Claire Blais* (1971). He is the editor of two anthologies of translations: *Stories from Québec* (1974) and *Voices from Québec* (1977). Currently he is working on a book to be entitled *All the Polarities*, a comparative study of English Canadian and Québécois works.

LORRAINE WEIR is Associate Professor of English at the University of British Columbia. She has published articles on Irish, British, and Canadian subjects and is currently working on two books, one on topography and language in modern Canadian poetry and another on Joycean grammatology — linguistic theories in and of the Joyce system.

GEORGE WOODCOCK is the author of numerous volumes including *Odysseus Ever Returning: Essays on Canadian Writers and Writing* (1970), *Peoples of the Coast* (1977), and *The World of Canadian Writing: Critiques and Recollections* (1980). In 1959 he founded *Canadian Literature: A Quarterly of Criticism and Review* and was its editor until 1977.

Index